Hero chimps

Remarkable tales of what they have done for us

by Julie Norton

Fourth edition October 2015 by Branchwood Publishing

© Copyright 2014. Julie Norton.

ISBN 978-1500476595

Contents

Giving chimps a voice

THE human species has demonstrated a starkly ambivalent attitude to chimpanzees, our closest evolutionary cousins. We can't seem to decide what relationship we should have with them. Are they a sub-species of homo sapiens, or merely unemotional, unthinking animals which just happen to look like funny versions of us?

Some of us regard them as amusing and endearing, like uncivilised clowns. But others have coldly used them for biomedical research or trained them in confined conditions for the entertainment industry. A few wealthy people have even nurtured them like proxy children.

Thousands of young chimps have been taken from their mothers and social groups to lead lives controlled by humans. Most of these individuals remain nameless and forgotten, but a few have gained celebrity status because of who their carers were, or because of their high profile environments. This book brings together the stories of these hero chimps, to bring attention to the way we have treated all their kind.

Bubbles, Michael Jackson's chimp-child, had the run of Neverland, but was sent away when a human child took his place. Washoe and Nim were taught sign language and proved they could think for themselves. Cheetah lived to the grand old age of 80, or did he? Was he just one of many 'actor' chimps used in the Tarzan films? Ham and Enos were highly intelligent chimps who were used mercilessly during the space race, then discarded when they had successfully paved the way for manned flight. London Zoo was the home to some messy young chimps who played the clown at tea-parties, but were they really enjoying themselves? A group of chimps was trained to 'act' in television adverts and helped increase the profits of a tea company, eventually being replaced by an unlikely woolly saviour.

These chimp biographies also highlight some hero humans who have done their utmost to halt the chimps' decline in the wild and provide a voice which these intelligent apes can't articulate for themselves.

JN

"Only if we understand can we care. Only if we care will we help. Only if we help shall they be saved."

Jane Goodall

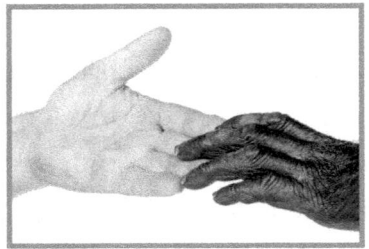

Bubbles

AFTER enjoying a close bond with a megastar 'parent' and a favoured life as a pampered chimp-child, Bubbles was unceremoniously given away when he grew too big and strong to handle.

When Bubbles was 'adopted' by Michael Jackson, the singer was one of the most famous and affluent people in the world. The chimp was surrounded by luxury at Neverland, the singer's famous 'theme park' home in California, until he was six or seven when he disappeared from public view. It was only when Jackson died in June 2009 that people wondered what had happened to the chimpanzee in the red suit who had been constantly photographed at Jackson's side a couple of decades earlier.

Distressing start

Like most captive chimps, Bubbles had a distressing start in life. According to most reports he was born in 1983 in a biomedical facility in Austin, Texas, where he was destined to be used for research. He escaped this fate when he was bought by animal trainer Bob Dunn, who then sold him on to Jackson when the chimp was eight months old.

This was Bubbles' third change of owner, and so far he had had

... he trusted animals more than people. Michael Jackson with Bubbles and a llama.

PHOTO BY SIPA PRESS/REX

no mother or close family to bond with. During the first year of life a chimp's emotional development echoes that of a human baby (though a new born chimp already has the motor skills of an average one-year-old human), and Bubbles would have desperately needed security and love. He evidently soon bonded with Jackson, seeing him as a parent figure, and by all accounts Jackson treated him well and gave him a stability and 'love' he had been lacking.

Free access

In 1988 Jackson, then 30, moved to Neverland where the chimp was allowed free access to all the rooms – a privilege not given to many adults around the singer. While it lasted, Bubbles' day-to-day life was as comfortable as it could be for a captive chimp. He was encouraged to use a toilet, was given gold-plated tyres to swing on and it was reported that he had his own personal chef. He also travelled extensively with Jackson, meeting film stars and celebrities, though many trips and events would undoubtedly have been stressful and confusing to a young chimp.

Jackson's sister La Toya, interviewed for a Channel 4 programme in 2010, said that Bubbles had "become one of us; he was just like a little kid". She said he had his own nanny and ate at the family table with a knife and fork. He opened the fridge and took food out; he took pyjamas out of a drawer, put them on and "said prayers". She described Jackson as a "surrogate mother" and said that Bubbles slept in his bed.[1]

Jackson would comb Bubbles' hair and in return the chimp would comb his owner's arm. (Chimps in the wild groom each other to cement social relationships and to establish their place in the group's hierarchy.)

Inseparable

La Toya said all the family loved Bubbles, and that Jackson and his chimp-son became inseparable.

On trips away from home Bubbles experienced the high life: he 'dined' with Elizabeth Taylor, sat in the studio while the *Bad* album was recorded, posed for fan pictures, appeared on television shows and 'attended' news conferences. And his likeness was used in a video game.

Jackson never brought Bubbles to Britain because of the quarantine laws, but when he was four years old the chimp flew first class with the singer and his entourage to Japan. While there he 'moonwalked' for the media, copying Jackson's famous dance. And it seems that Bubbles often received more attention than his celebrity owner. The Japanese consider monkeys to have special qualities (though Bubbles was an ape, not a monkey) and Bubbles had tea with the mayor, ate in restaurants and was generally treated like a VIP. However, he would nevertheless have found all this 'fame' confusing, missing his familiar surroundings and routine.

Chat shows

Back in the US, the public was also happy to see the chimp without Jackson. Bubbles took part in chat shows under the control of a trainer, and journalists were increasingly writing about the chimp, not his owner. Some observers thought this was a deliberate policy, as Jackson was now shunning attention unless he was performing on stage, and perhaps saw Bubbles as his 'representative'. There has been speculation that other, younger chimps were passed off as Bubbles after he grew too big, but Bubbles was the first, and by all accounts meant the most to Jackson.

According to the Center for Great Apes, where Bubbles now lives (at time of writing), Jackson bought at least two more chimps after

Bubbles was retired, called Max and Action Jackson (A.J.); there are a number of photos of Jackson with one of the later chimps, but they are all captioned 'Bubbles'.

The names of the other chimps were not made public and, according to the Center, one was eventually sold to a zoo in Korea and the other sent to a breeding farm in Kansas.

Unacceptable

By the 1980s attitudes were changing, particularly in the West, and it was becoming less acceptable to keep chimps as pets. Jackson was aware of growing criticism of his treatment of Bubbles, and he made the effort to contact chimp expert and conservationist, Jane Goodall. She acknowledged that he loved Bubbles in his own way, but gave him information about the plight of chimps and other great apes in the wild, in danger of becoming extinct because of deforestation and hunting, and Jackson was happy to publicise these issues.

Jackson's needy relationship with Bubbles can be more easily understood within the perspective of his own unnatural childhood. He was the youngest of nine children and was world famous by the age of nine. He commented that he used to have rehearsals every day after school while "other children played outside". By the time Jackson was 12 the Jackson Five had already had four number one hits and Michael, like his brothers, was working 15 hours a day and most nights. He was taught at home so had little opportunity to make friends outside the family. It was said he trusted animals more than people. When Jackson was a teenager he owned numerous pets including 13 rats, a boa constrictor and a python.

As his fame increased he said he felt like an animal in a cage with people always looking at him. He couldn't relate to normal people but animals provided company and were 'friends' who didn't know who he was and didn't criticise.

During an interview, clinical psychologist Dr Sari Shepphard said that Jackson and Bubbles used to make chimp noises to each other, and when Jackson hugged Bubbles the chimp would hug him back.

Jackson was so keen on eliciting a human response from Bubbles that he sought ways to teach the chimp to speak, and consulted various experts to find out how this might be achieved. He even asked a surgeon if he could perform an operation on Bubbles' vocal chords but was told the larynx is too high in a chimp's throat for speech as we know it. One account says he even surreptitiously brought a human brain preserved in a glass case back to the house, asking sister La Toya not to tell their mother.

'Poison' perfume

Despite all the evidence that Jackson treated Bubbles like a child, his brother Jermaine, writing in his book *You are not alone: Michael through a brother's eyes*, said that his younger brother's relationship with Bubbles was "no different" to that of "millions of dog and cat owners the world over". But Jermaine also recounts how Jackson gave Bubbles his own wardrobe and liberally covered the chimp in Dior's 'Poison' perfume. Jermaine added that Bubbles was better dressed than his (Jermaine's) own children.

Then around the late 1980s/early 1990s Bubbles' pampered life changed for ever. At the age of six or seven he was growing too big and strong to stay around people – a six-year-old chimp is stronger than an adult man – and, like so many captive chimps, his owner found him too unpredictable to handle.

So Bubbles was sent away from Neverland and the familiarity and security he had known, and for the next few years spent most of his time at Bob Dunn's training facility in California. He had one friend there, an older chimp called Sam. Initially Bubbles would have missed his familiar carers and surroundings and felt frightened and disorientated. He certainly wouldn't have had the freedom of movement he had enjoyed at Neverland.

During an interview, Bob Dunn said: "When chimps grow up, they become very strong and can weigh around 170 pounds. It's very hard to have to retire them, because you get so attached to them, it's just like telling your kid to go away."

Suitable

Then in March 2005 Bubbles was moved again, to the Center For Great Apes, about 200 miles north west of Miami. Bubbles and Sam arrived at the centre among a large group of chimps, all 'retired' from the entertainment world. The centre was also home to many other chimps and orangutans, all of whom had been rescued from unnatural lives. Most had been 'celebrities', and sanctuary founder and president Patti Ragan called them "The Hollywood Chimps".

The non profit-making sanctuary covers 120 acres and offers plenty of trees for the chimps and other apes to climb and swing on. The chimps live in large cupolas (domes) which connect to 4,000 feet of elevated tunnels, allowing them space and freedom.

When Bubbles first arrived, Ragan said he would not climb up to the top of his 35-foot tall cupola. He appeared to be nervous about the height and would sit on the ground and stare up at the other chimps while they played high above him. Baby chimps in the wild learn to climb by copying their mothers and other members of their family group, and they learn in stages as they are growing up – with a concerned mother looking on. Bubbles had never had another chimp to show him how.

Courage

When he had been at the sanctuary for about five months, Bubbles suddenly found courage and climbed to the top of the cupola. Ragan said he was so pleased and excited that he gave a loud chimp call. Now it's one of his favourite places and he goes to the top to play several times a day.

Ragan added: "Bubbles can be sensitive and dramatic. If he has any kind of cut or scratch on his body – no matter how small – he will show it many times during the day to his caregivers and ask for sympathy." She said Bubbles and his new family have a stress-free existence: "They relax. They take naps together. They go out in the chutes and lie under a tree in the tunnel system. They groom each other and they fight and have arguments too!" However, old habits die hard, and she says that Bubbles still likes making faces for the camera.

She said: "Bubbles has a broad, handsome face and a lot of charisma; he's healthy and good natured. Though he is able to throw sand with amazing accuracy, he is extremely gentle with the youngsters. He is very connected and happy in his chimpanzee family. He's a very dignified chimp. Everyone remembers him as the pink-eared, pink-faced chimp in the red suit. But the world has missed his adolescence and adulthood."

At time of writing Bubbles weighed 185 pounds, was about 4½ feet tall and was the dominant male in a group of chimpanzees at the sanctuary

He is still owned by Jackson's estate, and is the only great ape at the sanctuary who is not owned by the Center. However, the Center says that Jackson did not include Bubbles in his will as some have claimed, and although Jackson was unquestionably fond of Bubbles, he never once visited him at the sanctuary. Ragan said that despite the time lapse Bubbles probably would have recognized him.

She said: "Most of our chimps recognize their former owners. They get very excited to see them and I am sure Bubbles would have recognized Jackson.

Jackson's sister, La Toya, did visit Bubbles in 2010. She was filmed and interviewed and asked how she had felt about Bubbles being taken away from the family home. She said: "Animals have to grow up. That's life."

Jackson died in 2009 when Bubbles was 26 years old. Ragan said: "There were over 90 requests that year by media organisations to come and film Bubbles, but we only allowed two in six months: Anderson Cooper of CNN and the *Today Show* in July 2009. We are working hard to protect the apes' peace and privacy."

A 'biography' of Bubbles was published by John Blake, called *My Secret Diary, From Swaziland to Neverland*, described as a "collection of very personal and honest entries from Bubbles' 'diary'", giving the "whole story" of the chimp's life. The book describes how he escaped from an "awful childhood" in a research clinic, and "adopted

11

a struggling young singer". Luckily, in real life Bubbles has managed to escape to a happy, caring new home.

[1] (p5) Bubbles wasn't alone in closely observing human behaviour. A home-raised chimp called Lucy, the subject of a book called *Lucy, Growing Up Human* by her 'father', Maury Temerlin, intrigued primatologist, Jane Goodall. She writes: "I watched, amazed, as she opened the refrigerator and various cupboards, found bottles and a glass, then poured herself a gin and tonic. She took the drink to the TV, turned the set on, flipped from one channel to another then, as though in disgust, turned it off again. She selected a glossy magazine from the table, and still carrying her drink, settled in a comfortable chair."

• The earliest known account of a chimpanzee being treated as a human child is of a baby chimp taken on board a ship travelling from Angola to England in the late 17th century. The crew became fond of it, dressed it in clothes, gave it their food at table and a bed with blankets at night. The chimp survived only two months before becoming infected after a fall on board. (Courtesy BBC.)

" If we look straight and deep into a chimpanzee's eyes, an intelligent self-assured personality looks back at us. If they are animals, what must we be?"

Frans de Waal

Washoe and Nim Chimpsky

THIS is a complicated tale of two individuals who were exploited by their human carers in a bid to prove chimps could communicate using sign language. Washoe fared better than Nim, who was handed from carer to teacher to carer, to a biomedical laboratory, then to a sanctuary for rescued horses. But both chimps were essentially used as pawns in an intellectual game of linguistics.

As Michael Jackson discovered (see p8), the larynx is too high in a chimp's throat to facilitate oral speech as we know it, but researchers have been keen to demonstrate that chimps are primed to communicate and will learn sign language given the right method and environment. Washoe and Nim took part in separate experiments at different times, run by scientists who vied with each other to prove their results were the definitive ones.

Washoe

Washoe was claimed to be the first non-human to learn to communicate using American Sign Language (ASL), as part of a research experiment on animal language acquisition. She learned approximately 350 words of ASL and passed some words on to her adopted son Loulis (she had lost two of her own babies and became a surrogate mother to him). Loulis consequently learned sign language in a natural way: from his mother, and without human intervention.

Washoe was born in West Africa in 1965. Like Ham and Enos (see page 43) she was captured for the US Air Force and destined to be used in research for the space programme.

But when Washoe was 10 months old she was handed over to husband and wife scientists, Allen and Beatrix Gardner, who established a project to teach her ASL at the University of Nevada, Reno (her name was taken from Washoe County, Nevada). Previous attempts to teach chimps to imitate vocal languages had failed because of the position of their larynx. When communicating in the wild chimps use a mixture of body gestures (further research has now been done: see page 90), so the Gardners believed this tendency would lend itself to teaching Washoe ASL.

Companionship

As part of the project the couple treated Washoe like their own child, aiming to satisfy her psychological need for family and companionship. Just like Michael Jackson's Bubbles, she frequently wore clothes and sat with the Gardners at the dinner table. Washoe had the use of her own 8 x 24 foot trailer, with a couch, drawers, refrigerator and a bed with sheets and blankets. She had access to clothing, combs, toys, books and a toothbrush. She was given a regular routine of chores, outdoor play and rides in the family car. On one outing Washoe saw a swan and signed *water* and *bird*; the Gardners were happily reassured that the project was working.

According to the book *Next of Kin* by Roger Fouts and Stephen Tukel Mills, the Gardners wanted Washoe to acquire more than merely a vocabulary. They believed that she was not a passive laboratory subject but a primate endowed with a powerful need to learn and communicate. The Gardners wanted Washoe "to ask questions, to comment on what we did, and to stimulate our conversation". They wanted her to have true two-way communication with humans.

Washoe also had the stimulus of four other regular human carers, whose role was to give her emotional attention as well as monitor her progress.

But, like all chimps, Washoe became bigger and harder to control, and when she was five the Gardners decided to move her to the University of Oklahoma's Institute of Primate Studies in Norman, Oklahoma. There Washoe continued to learn sign language under the care of American primate researcher, Roger Fouts and his wife Deborah; Fouts had been tutored by Allen Gardner, and considered that Washoe had been "part stepchild and part research subject" with the Gardners. But at the Institute she was now one of a group of chimps being studied, and at first she was confused and stressed to mix with other chimps when she had known only the company of humans. Eventually she settled and made friends with her own kind.

Less confusing

Both the Gardners and the Fouts were careful to communicate with Washoe only in ASL, avoiding vocal communication, as they felt this would create a less confusing learning environment. This technique is commonly used when teaching human children how to sign. Washoe was rewarded with food or with tickling[1].

Then the scientists discovered that Washoe could also pick up ASL gestures by observing humans around her who were signing amongst themselves. For example, when a couple of researchers signed **toothbrush** to each other while they brushed their teeth near Washoe, she showed no indication of having noticed, but on a later occasion she saw a toothbrush and spontaneously produced the correct sign, demonstrating that she had in fact previously observed and learned the sign.

Changed strategy

The researchers then realised that rewarding particular signs with food and tickles was actually interfering with the chimps using sign language conversationally, so they changed their strategy. They avoided instruction at meal times and they stopped the tickle rewards because these tended to result in the chimps collapsing into giggles. Instead, they set up an environment that encouraged communication without the use of rewards for specific actions. It was deemed that a sign was truly learned only when a chimp used it spontaneously and appropriately for 14 consecutive days.

Washoe and her fellow chimps were able to combine the hundreds of signs they had learned into novel combinations, which they hadn't been taught, but created themselves with different meanings. For instance, when a chimp called Moja didn't know the word for "thermos", he referred to it as a **metal cup drink**[2].

When carers were absent for a long period it was noticed that Washoe would ignore them on their return, as a form of chastisement. One carer, Kat, had a miscarriage and missed work for many weeks and, according to Roger Fouts, on her return Washoe gave her the "cold shoulder".

He said: "Kat decided to 'tell' Washoe the truth, signing **my baby** *died*." Washoe stared at Kat then peered into her eyes and carefully signed *cry*, touching Kat's cheek and drawing a finger down the path a tear would make on a human (chimps don't produce tears). Kat later remarked that this one sign told her more about Washoe's mental capabilities than all the chimp's longer, grammatically perfect sentences.

When Washoe was shown an image of herself in the mirror and was asked what it was, she replied: *Me, Washoe*. She also enjoyed playing with dolls, which she would talk to, bathe and act out imaginary scenarios.

Humbling

When new students came to work with Washoe, it was reported that she would recognise that they were novices and slow down her rate of signing, which had a humbling effect on them.

In 1980 Washoe, her adopted son Loulis and Moja moved with the Fouts to the newly formed Chimpanzee and Human Communication Institute at Central Washington University in Ellensburg. They stayed there until May 1993 when Washoe, Loulis and other chimps were moved again, this time to specially constructed accommodation located within the campus of the university.

Fouts commented: "This was the culmination of 15 years of planning, including 10 years of fundraising, eight years of designing, and two years of building, to give the chimps a more natural home. They could now enjoy life in a grassy area of more than five thousand square feet, which provided giant climbing poles and structures, earthen terraces, and hanging fire hoses, all enclosed in a wire fence dome that reached 32 feet above the ground."

To prepare the chimps for their new home, volunteers had produced a videotape preview. Two days before the move, Washoe and the other chimps gathered around a television set to watch. One of the volunteers signed to them what the new facilities would be like, including: ***Look! Door there - you can go out! See grass. You can run, climb, play. You will love new house house! We all go with you!*** Apparently the chimps were entranced and when the tape was finished, they asked to see it again[3].

Having enjoyed many years in a natural environment with others of her own kind, Washoe died in October 2007 at the age of 42.

[1] (p15) The Gardners expanded on chimps' reactions to tickling in *Teaching Sign Language to a Chimpanzee* (August 1969): "Anyone who becomes familiar with a young chimpanzee soon learns about their passion for being tickled. There is no doubt that tickling is the most effective reward that we have used with Washoe. In the early months when we would pause in our tickling, Washoe would indicate that she wanted more tickling by taking our hands and placing them against her ribs or around her neck."

[2] (p16) In her book *Through A Window* Jane Goodall discusses the belief that chimps who have learnt sign language can make up their own words. She says: "Washoe puzzled her caretakers by asking repeatedly for a ***rock berry***. Eventually it transpired that she was referring to brazil nuts which she had [just] encountered." Goodall said another sign-trained chimp described a cucumber as a ***green banana*** and an Alka Seltzer as a ***listen drink***.

[3] (This page) In *Next of Kin: My Conversations with Chimpanzees* Fouts described the reaction of a chimp called Dar to the new compound: "Dar squeezed by and exploded out the door and down the stairs to the ground. He raced across the grass field with such an ecstatic movement that he looked like he was skipping, quadrupedally. He headed directly for the far terrace, climbed to the top of the 32-foot high fence, and gazed out over Ellensburg. Then he turned toward us and let out a loud pant-hoot of happiness."

Nim Chimpsky

In 1973 a chimp called Nim Chimpsky became the subject of a further study involving signing. Called Project Nim, it was headed by behavioural psychologist Herbert Terrace at Columbia University. The chimp's name was a pun on Noam Chomsky, an expert on human language structure, who believed that humans were "wired" to develop language, but that chimps were not. Terrace set up the study as a challenge to Chomsky's thesis; he wanted Project Nim to go further than Project Washoe and aimed to use more rigorous experimental techniques so that the linguistic abilities of chimps could be more clearly analysed.

Sceptical

Fouts believed that the results were not as impressive as those from the Washoe project. Terrace, on the other hand, was sceptical of Project Washoe and, according to his critics, went to great lengths to discredit it. He and his researchers argued that the chimp's ability to learn to sign may have amounted to nothing more than a "Clever Hans"[1] effect, combined with a relatively informal experimental approach. For example, "man bites dog" and "dog bites man" both use the same set of words but, because of their different order, will be understood by a human as having very different meanings, but not necessarily by a chimp.

The project started in November 1973 when Nim was only two

weeks old. He was taken abruptly from his mother, Caroline, one of many chimps living at the Institute for Primate Studies in Oklahoma, where Dr William Lemmon was director. Terrace handed Nim over to Stephanie Lafarge, a former student, and instructed her to take the chimp into her own home and mother him.

In the film *Project Nim*[2] Lafarge referred to the trauma experienced by the mother: "She knew what was going to happen. She'd had six of her previous babies removed in the same way. Dr Lemmon shot her with a tranquilising gun and said: 'Quick, we need to get him before she falls over and falls on him.' Nim didn't struggle, didn't try to get away, he just screamed, clinging and attaching [to Lafarge] for dear life."

Lafarge's was a crowded and chaotic home environment. She had recently married and between her and husband Wer they were bringing up seven children within a hippie environment. Nim became close and dependent on Lafarge, while becoming aggressive towards Wer.

Lafarge said: "Terrace told me to bring Nim into my home and raise this infant as if he were a child, to see if he would acquire language from being part of a family. I knew nothing about chimpanzees; I never sat down to study them as I should have perhaps. The fact that we could share language with an animal seemed a radical possibility at that time.

Breastfed

"I breastfed him for a couple months. It seemed completely natural, but I wasn't prepared for the wild animal in him."

If Wer put his arm round his wife Nim would bite him on the arm, leaving Wer feeling excluded.

Terrace thought it might diffuse the situation by introducing another teacher into the equation, so Laura-Ann Petitto was hired to help teach Nim sign language, necessitating regular visits to the house. But this caused rivalry between the two women.

Petitto said of Nim's home environment: "This was utter chaos for a scientific project. [Nim] was given puffs on a joint, and alcohol. I thought there is something wrong here. This was not the way you'd teach a child language."

Classroom

Then Terrace decided to try removing Nim from Lafarge's house during the day to a classroom he set up at Columbia University, and Petitto commented that Nim's signing then increased "exponentially". Nim even invented his own sign for *play*: clapping his hands together.

Examples of the word groups Nim learnt include: *Banana Nim eat*; *Hug me Nim*; *Play me Nim*; *Tickle me Nim*; *Tickle me eat*; *Banana eat me Nim*; *Eat drink eat drink*; *Grape eat me Nim*; *Me eat drink more*; *Tickle me Nim play*. In an article *How Nim Chimpsky Changed My Mind*, Terrace gives Nim's longest sentence as having 16 words: *Give orange me give eat orange me eat orange give me eat orange give me you*.

The relationship between Nim's two carers continued to deteriorate and Terrace decided to move the chimp right away from the Lafarge family. Lafarge commented: "My separation was just as abrupt as [Nim's] from his mother."

Nim's new home was the Delafield Estate in Riverdale, New York. He was growing stronger and his aggression was becoming a problem to his carers; he would bite when upset. Terrace commented: "He could size someone up in two seconds – whether they were confident or secretly unconfident."

Nim then had to endure many changes of carer. Joyce Butler joined the team and had to suffer Nim's bites when he wasn't happy. She said: "I didn't know the difference between a chimp and a monkey. I was blind and ignorant." In a natural environment Nim would have

"Grape eat me Nim"

Nim's signing then increased "exponentially".

COMPOSITE ILLUSTRATION BY REDROOSTER DIGITAL DESIGN (WWW.REDROOSTER.TV)

been testing his aggressive personality on other males, learning what his limits were and where he fitted in the group hierarchy. His human 'family' were unable to react to him in a natural chimp way.

Petitto then fell out with Terrace and reluctantly abandoned the experiment. She said: "It was the humans I wanted to leave, not the chimp."

She was replaced by Renee Talitz who found it difficult to teach Nim in his 'classroom' at the university: "It was a dungeon, 15 feet square with no windows. It was difficult to get Nim's attention, he'd rather do something else. He was getting smarter and smarter, taking advantage of situations." Reminiscent of a bored human child at school, Nim would constantly sign *toilet* to get them both out of the room. On one occasion he became aggressive and bit through Talitz's cheek.

Damage

Nim's volatile character was making it increasingly difficult to pursue the language experiment and Terrace decided to bring it to a halt earlier than planned. He said: "No-one keeps a chimp for more than five years because they don't know their own strength and they can do a lot of damage to people. We had reams of data but couldn't continue scientifically. Can a chimp create a sentence? I don't think I had any definitive conclusion to that."

So Nim was transported back to the Institute for Primate Studies in Oklahoma. Terrace said: "I thought the surroundings in which he was born would provide the most psychological support for Nim. His basic needs would be taken care of."

Many observers felt this was heartless, given the life Nim had led surrounded by human company and stimulus. It was as if he had been discarded, returned to a strictly research environment where his home was now a cage with no daylight. And up to that point he had never seen another chimp. Terrace did admit that the facility was more "primitive" than he remembered.

Terrace visited Nim only once, a year later for a photo shoot, and the chimp rushed to greet him like an old friend. Observers said that Nim was devastated; seeing Terrace, he assumed that he had come to take him 'home'. Terrace described Nim as an "organism, almost like communicating with a creature from outer space".

Then Nim found a champion. Bob Ingersoll, a research student

"… Can a chimp create a sentence? I don't think I had any definitive conclusion to that."

at the Institute, felt indignant on Nim's behalf that he had been abandoned to a "prison" environment where the chimp was shut in a cage with a chain around his neck. He commented: "It looked like an ugly dark dank prison. Nim trusted us. He was going to come back and be celebrated [as] the great signing chimp. Exactly the opposite. Nim in a cage. No special treatment. No yogurt, no granola, none of that. Pretty traumatic for the chimp."

Stranger

Then Ingersoll noticed a stranger at the Institute making notes about Nim and the other chimps. This was Dr James Mahoney from the Laboratory for Experimental Medicine Surgery in Primates (LEMSIP), a pharmaceutical animal testing laboratory where chimps were used to test vaccines for Hepatitis B and C, HIV and Aids. Ingersoll said: "He represented the Devil to me."

Dr Lemmon was having financial problems keeping the Institute for Primate Studies running and LEMSIP had offered to buy some of the chimps.

Mahoney said: "I had to choose which chimps for which kind of research. There's no way you can carry out research on animals and for it to be humane. It can't be humane because you've already put them in a cage. From there on it's downhill."

Key words

Nim and other chimps were relocated to LEMSIP and researchers there were surprised to see that the chimps were continuing to sign to each other. So they decided to utilise this in a positive way. They wrote key words and their equivalent signs on pieces of paper attached to the walls of the lab so that people could understand what the chimps were trying to say and at the same time learn the signs themselves.

Meanwhile Ingersoll campaigned for Nim's release: "I made a big stink about it in every way I could. I called the press." Mahoney complained that Ingersoll would hound him at every opportunity: "then it dawned on me that he was the only one who cared [about Nim]".

Then Ingersoll's campaigning alerted the attention of lawyer Henry Herrmann: "Someone at the *Boston Globe* told me to read the front page story that day." The headline read: *Hard times for bright chimp* next to a photo of Terrace with Nim.

Herrmann was struck by Nim's plight and decided to instigate a court case against LEMSIP. He said: "I thought it was a unique esoteric form of animal cruelty and as a lawyer I thought it was just plain illegal if the young chimp had been brought up from infancy in a family. You can't stick him in a little cage in some horrible medical lab and use him for experiments. Early on I decided that if this animal has deliberately been brought up from infanthood to think of himself as human then if I'm going to represent him I have to treat him like a human client. Give him his day in court."

Let him talk

Ingersoll and Herrmann collaborated on Nim's behalf. Ingersoll said: "Henry had a really cool strategy; he said: 'Hey this chimp can speak for himself. Let's bring him into court and let him talk'."

Herrmann planned to bring a steel cage containing Nim into court as a trial exhibit with "a couple of strong guys with a pole ready to carry it into court, and get Nim to go into a frenzy and signal **out, out, out**."

However, the judge emphatically ruled out that scenario, saying he wouldn't have a mockery made of the court. But the damage was done; Ingersoll pointed out that the media attention would have been devastating for LEMSIP: "And the demon medical factory said:

"... 'Hey this chimp can speak for himself. Let's bring him into court and let him talk'."

COMPOSITE ILLUSTRATION BY REDROOSTER DIGITAL DESIGN (WWW.REDROOSTER.TV)

'That's it, get that chimp out of here'".

All this publicity around Nim caught the attention of the late Cleveland Amory, a prominent author and animal rights advocate from the Fund for Animals, who ran the Black Beauty Ranch in Murchison, Texas, a sanctuary predominantly for retired and abused horses and donkeys.

Highly publicised rescue

In April 1983 Amory and The Fund conducted a highly publicised rescue of Nim. Amory proclaimed: "I'm saving Nim; he will live here for the rest of his natural life."

But Ingersoll was critical of Amory, because: "he didn't know a thing about chimps", and because Nim would be the only chimp on the ranch. Nim was in fact the only animal the ranch had ever bought.

Amory built a house for Nim with a porch so he could go outside, and gave him toys, but Ingersoll was worried about him being solitary and pointed out: "Chimps are social animals. You can't just put one chimp in a box and expect everything to be cool."

To give Nim the illusion of company Amory fixed a TV set up high so the chimp could see people and activity, but Nim knocked it down and broke it.

Ingersoll wrote to Cleveland voicing his worries and pointing out that leaving the sociable Nim there alone was "virtually torture". This didn't please Cleveland and he threatened to arrest Ingersoll if he came to the ranch.

Nim's early carer Lafarge visited the chimp. He recognised her and she foolishly insisted on going into his enclosure. He grabbed her by the ankle and swung her around, banging her against a wall. She managed to get out intact and admitted: "So much damage was done removing him from what his life should have been. We exploited his human-like nature without regard to his chimp-like nature."

It would be 10 years before Ingersoll could visit Nim. Chris Burn had then taken over the ranch and welcomed Ingersoll, reassuring him that under his care life would be better for the lone chimp. Despite the long time lapse Nim immediately recognised Ingersoll and signed *play*.

In 1995 LEMSIP closed and Ingersoll managed to arrange for two more chimps to join Nim, an unaggressive male and a female both of whom Nim had known at the lab. Ingersoll became a regular visitor to the ranch; of Nim's situation he said: "Things were as good as could be expected. It wasn't perfect but pretty damn good."

The three chimps successfully bonded and were companions for the five years before Nim died of a heart attack in May 2000 aged 26.

Did Washoe and Nim use language?

Although Nim eventually learned 125 signs, Terrace concluded that Nim had not learned anything worthy of the name "language" (as defined by Noam Chomsky). He said that Nim's 'speech' was strictly pragmatic, as a means of obtaining an outcome, unlike a human child, who uses language to express meanings, thoughts or ideas.

Terrace ultimately dismissed the whole project and pronounced that there was nothing Nim could be taught that could not equally well be taught to a pigeon using the principles of operant conditioning. Petitto agreed with him and estimated that with more standard criteria, Nim's true vocabulary count was closer to 25 than 125. But other observers and teachers disagreed and criticised the way that Terrace had conducted his experiment. Some said that Terrace used his analysis to discredit the movement of ape-language research in general.

Terrace's conclusions also led to heated disputes with the Gardners who had carried out the Washoe experiment. They argued that Terrace's approach to Nim's training, including the fact that the chimp had had a succession of different teachers, had hindered his cognitive and linguistic abilities. Roger Fouts agreed and described Project Nim as poorly conducted. He said that the process of acquiring language skills through natural social interaction gives substantially better results than behavioural conditioning, which can lead to the use of language as a method mainly of getting rewards.

In an interview with Ryan Lambie in 2011 Ingersoll gave his opinion: "I think that it may be true that [Nim] didn't use sentences and grammar, in the sense that this verb goes before that adverb, and this noun goes here and not there. But I think it would be ridiculous to think that ... you'd hand this being, that's millions of years' divergent from us in terms of evolution, twenty terms and then a dictionary, and immediately hear grammatically correct sentences."

[1] (p19) Clever Hans (*Kluge Hans* in German) was an Orlov Trotter breed of horse which was claimed to have been able to perform arithmetic and other intellectual tasks. In 1907 psychologist Oskar Pfungst demonstrated that the horse was not actually performing these mental tasks, but was watching the reaction of his human observers. He discovered that the horse was responding directly to involuntary cues in the body language of the human trainer.

[2] (p20) Quotes and some reporting are from *Project Nim*, a documentary film by James Marsh Films based on a book by Elizabeth Hess called *Chimpsky, the chimp who would be human*. It explored Terrace's experiments and theories, considered

ethical issues and the emotional experiences of both Nim and his teachers, using the people involved or actors representing them to voice their experiences of the project. The documentary was produced by BBC Films and the UK Film Council, in association with HBO Documentary Films, Red Box Films and Passion Pictures. It opened the 2011 Sundance Film Festival. (Peter Bradshaw wrote a review of the film in the *Guardian* newspaper, where he concluded: "The chimp comes out of it well. Homo sapiens, of course, is found wanting.")

Learning language via a keyboard

KANZI, a male bonobo, exhibited advanced linguistic aptitude, according to primatologist, Sue Savage-Rumbaugh.

Born in October 1980 at Emory University, Kanzi was 'stolen' from his natural mother and 'adopted' shortly after birth by a dominant female, Matata, who was being taught language through keyboard lexigrams.

Kanzi accompanied Matata to the lessons at the Language Research Center at Georgia State University but apparently showed little interest at first. However, one day in Matata's absence, Kanzi began competently using the lexigrams, so becoming the first observed ape to have learned aspects of language naturalistically rather than through direct training.

Kanzi soon mastered the ten words the researchers had been struggling to teach his adoptive mother, and went on to learn more than two hundred. When he heard a spoken word (through headphones, to filter out non-verbal clues), he pointed to the correct lexigram.

The chimp also picked up some American Sign Language from watching videos of Koko, a gorilla who communicated with her keeper using sign language; Kanzi signed **You, Gorilla, Question** to anthropologist Dawn Prince-Hughes, who had previously worked closely with gorillas.

It was also noticed that every time he communicated using graphic symbols, he also produced some vocalisation. Researchers pointed out that Kanzi was actually producing the articulate equivalent of the symbols he was indicating, albeit in a distorted manner.

Equal with humans

THE groundbreaking work with signing primates led to the foundation of the Great Ape Project, which aims to "include the non-human great apes [chimpanzees, orangutans and gorillas] within the community of equals by granting them the basic moral and legal protections that only humans currently enjoy", in order to place them in the moral category of "persons" rather than private property.

"We admit that we are like apes, but we seldom realise that we are apes."

Richard Dawkins

Cheetah - or was he?

CONFUSION abounds around Cheetah, the chimp who 'acted' alongside Johnny Weissmuller in the MGM Tarzan films of the early 20th century. Some say that he was 80 years old when he died. Can that be true? And did the same chimp 'star' in more than 50 films?

An 80-year-old chimpanzee died of kidney failure on Christmas Eve 2011 at The Suncoast Primate Sanctuary in Palm Harbour, Florida, his demise setting off much discussion and argument as to whether he was actually the chimp he was claimed to be. Was this really Cheetah, the chimp who starred in the MGM Tarzan films during the 1930s and 1940s, alongside Johnny Weissmuller and Maureen O'Sullivan? If he was then he would indeed have been around 80 years old as claimed, an unlikely age for a chimp to reach.

Until the news of Cheetah's death it was unheard of for a chimp to live as long as this, but many people believed this was true, and Cheetah was listed in *The Guinness Book of Records* as the world's oldest non-human primate.

But when Cheetah's death was announced it was claimed that the genuine Cheeta (spelt without an 'h') was living at a different sanctuary, the C.H.E.E.T.A. Primate Foundation in Palm Springs; and that he was not just alive and well but painting 'Ape-stract' pictures for his adoring public.

And to confuse matters further, some Hollywood accounts indicate that there was also a chimp called Jiggs or Mr Jiggs who played Cheetah in the early Tarzan films, and that this individual died of pneumonia aged nine in February 1938 and was buried in the Los Angeles Pet Cemetery.

Raised by apes

The Tarzan films were based on books written by Edgar Rice Burroughs and relate the adventures of a man who was raised by apes in Africa. However, the Cheetah character was created especially for the films and did not appear in the original books. MGM decided to add the part of a chimp as a friend for Tarzan to make the films more appealing and add a humorous twist to the stories. MGM was proved right, as the character of Cheetah, who appeared in around 50 films altogether, turned out to be one of the most popular movie animal stars, matching Rin Tin Tin or Asta, the dog from the Thin Man movies.

Film historian and Turner Classic Movies host, Robert Osbourne said Cheetah's character "was one of the things people loved about the Tarzan movies because he made people laugh. He was always a regular fun part of the movies."

It is undisputable that several different chimps were used during the run of the Tarzan films. MGM would have wanted to perpetuate the myth that the chimp so loved by the film-going public was always the same one (it is widely accepted that several dogs were trained for the part of Rin Tin Tin).

Only young chimps would have been pliable enough to withstand the rigours of training and filming without becoming too aggressive to 'act' alongside humans, and risking the safety of lucrative film stars. And it is likely that the different owners of the various chimps would have been vying with each other to claim theirs was the genuine 'star'.

According to *Washington Post* journalist R. D. Rosen: "In each Tarzan movie, the Cheeta role [was] played by more than one chimp, depending on what talents the scene called for."

Urban legend

And when Cheetah's death was announced it was reported in the *Daily Telegraph* that Eve Golden, a film historian at the Everett Collection, a Hollywood archive, said: "There doesn't seem to be any verification that this particular chimp was ever really in any movies or television shows at all. I think it's just an urban legend. Unless they have the chimpanzee's acting union card it seems impossible to prove."

The original Cheetah chimp is believed to have been born in the Liberian jungle and taken as a baby from his mother by an animal trainer in April 1932 (almost undoubtedly this means his mother, if not other members of his family, would have been killed in order to capture the baby: it is estimated that the removal of one infant will result in the death of up to ten other chimps).

The chimp's first film role was as an 'extra' in *Tarzan and His Mate* in 1934, before he was given the name Cheetah in *Tarzan Escapes* in 1936, 'acting' alongside Tarzan, played by Johnny Weissmuller (previously an American Olympic gold medal swimmer). Cheetah then went on to appear in another 12 Tarzan films (the role most likely shared among several young chimps). If the Cheetah who died in 2011 was the original one, he certainly outlived his fellow actors: Johnny Weissmuller died in 1984 aged 79, and Maureen O'Sullivan, who played Tarzan's mate Jane, died in 1998 aged 87.

Cheetah's last role is said to have been as Chee-Chee in the 1967 musical film *Doctor Doolittle* starring Rex Harrison, but it would have been highly unlikely if not unique that the original chimp would still have been 'acting' in his thirties.

Chimps in the wild can live for 40 to 50 years, though those in captivity often live a lot longer, benefiting from regular nourishment, medical attention (the Palm Springs Cheetah was given insulin for diabetes) plus the absence of predators and threats from aggressive rivals.

The genuine one?

Debbie Cobb, outreach director at the Suncoast Primate Sanctuary, was adamant that the Cheetah who died in 2011 was the genuine one. She insisted that the chimp had lived there for about 50 years, her grandparents having acquired him in about 1960 from Johnny Weissmuller's estate, and that the chimp had appeared in Tarzan films between 1932 and 1934. But she was unable to produce any proof at the time of Cheetah's death. She said: "Unfortunately, there was a fire in 1995 in which a lot of that documentation burned up. I've known him for 51 years. My first memory of him coming here was when I was actually five, and I've known him ever since, and he was a full-grown chimp then."

She told the *Tampa Tribune* that Cheetah was an outgoing chimp who loved fingerpainting, football and "non-denominational Christian music". She added: "He was very compassionate. He could tell if I was having a good day or a bad day. He was always trying to get me to laugh if he thought I was having a bad day," She said Cheetah was not a troublemaker, although he had been known to throw his own faeces if he became upset.

Or was it Cheeta?

Meanwhile the other 'film star' Cheeta, living at the C.H.E.E.T.A. (Creative Habitats and Enrichment for Endangered and Threatened Apes) Primate Foundation in Palm Springs, was given paints and brushes and encouraged to use them. The result was 'Ape-stract' paintings which were sold to raise money for primate charities. It was reported that his 'expressionistic' paintings were even displayed in London's National Gallery. Cheeta apparently also 'watched' television, including the old Tarzan films, with his grandson Jeeter (who inherited the role of resident artist). He also 'read' books and 'played' the piano.

His main carer was Dan Westfall, who founded the sanctuary in April 1991, its aim to provide a caring home for ex-showbusiness apes and monkeys.

Westfall said primatologist Jane Goodall inspired him to create the sanctuary, and that it had adopted Cheeta's name to highlight the fact that animals used in the entertainment industry were sometimes abused or even killed while being used as 'props'.

Elusive

So the true facts about Cheetah or Cheeta are elusive. After Cheetah's death author James Lever said: "Nobody seems to know very much about the chimps who played Cheetah. I rather think he'll be dying a lot over the next few years."

Lever wrote a spoof biography, *Me Cheeta*, published in 2008, an account of Cheeta's long 'career' in Hollywood, including his supposed 'comments' on his fellow stars and celebrities. He was 'quoted' as saying:

"I acted into my thirties. Most chimps retire by the age of ten because they won't do what they're told. I didn't want to end up in a lab with an electrode in my forehead."

"The art world credits me with starting Ape-stract painting, but I don't like to blow my own trumpet. I prefer the piano."

"My only vices are hamburgers and caffeine-free Coke. Fresh fruit, vegetables and monkey chow are the key."

Palm Springs Cheeta with Dan Westfall. An 'Ape-stract' painting can be seen on the left.

PHOTO BY KEYSTONE USA-ZUM/REX SHUTTERSTOCK

Campaign

Me Cheeta was longlisted for the Man Booker Prize and prompted Cheeta fans to campaign, unsuccessfully, over the internet for the chimp to receive a BAFTA award for a long lifetime of entertaining humans. The campaign was supported by many celebrities, but BAFTA chief executive, Amanda Berry, said: "I'm afraid that, although [Cheeta is] clearly a much-loved figure within the film industry and the viewing public at large, the Academy does not currently recognise the work of animals."

The Palm Springs Cheeta was honoured with a star on the Palm Springs Walk of Stars in 1995, but there have been several subsequent unsuccessful campaigns, including one by film maker Matt Devlen, to secure a star for the chimp on the Hollywood Walk of Fame. And there was an online petition to get supporters to urge the Hollywood Chamber of Commerce to give him a star in 2009.

Although no-one knows exactly when Cheeta was born, his 'birthdays' were regularly celebrated. In 2006, when he was said to be 74, Cheeta received an award from the International Film Festival of Peniscola Comedy and was honoured by a visit from Jane Goodall. A report of his 75th birthday was published in *National Geographic*, and his 76th was celebrated in April 2008 at his house 'Casa de Cheeta' in Palm Springs, at an event hosted by Dan Westfall and Diane Weissmuller, the widow of Johnny Weissmuller's son. The press and many celebrities attended.

Temperamental

According to the Palm Springs sanctuary, Cheeta was an outgoing chimp who loved humans. Yet not everyone thought so. Maureen

O'Sullivan played Jane in six Tarzan movies and, according to her daughter, actor Mia Farrow, the chimp could often be temperamental. She once said via Twitter: "My mom invariably referred to Cheeta as 'that bastard'."

Cheeta was subject to an exposé as a fake in 2008 by journalist R. D. Rosen. He said that he had discovered that this particular chimp was born in 1960 or 1961 and had never been in a Tarzan film. The C.H.E.E.T.A. Primate Foundation now admits on its website that their Cheeta is unlikely to be as old as they thought and that "it is also difficult to determine which movies, if any, our Cheeta may have been in. As a result of this discovery, we updated our website to reflect the information putting Cheeta's life history in doubt. It appears that the facts of our Cheeta's past will almost certainly remain a Hollywood mystery."

Jane Goodall commented: "Cheeta is the ambassador for all the chimps that played "'Cheeta'".

Whichever chimp was the real Cheetah the fact remains that several young chimps were trained to behave like clowning humans in Tarzan films at the beginning of last century, and at least two chimps lived to a grand old age, leading unnatural if not unhappy lives in US sanctuaries. They all deserve to be remembered as heroes.

"We must, however, acknowledge, as it seems to me, that man with all his noble qualities... still bears in his bodily frame the indelible stamp of his lowly origin."

Charles Darwin

Ham, Enos and the space chimps

CHIMPS acting as astronauts might sound amusing and fascinating; imagining a chimp in a space suit peering through a cockpit window is likely to raise a smile. But the historical truth reveals a different, unsettling picture. The story of Ham, Enos, and the innumerable other young chimps used in the space race highlights our ambivalent attitude to our close cousin: we justified using them for extreme experimentation in space because we didn't want to risk the lives of humans; but paradoxically chimps were chosen because they are so similar to us.

The 'space race' between the United States and the Soviet Union began in earnest just after the Second World War, with neither country co-operating or sharing research with the other, and with both aiming to be the first to propel a human up into space.

From the late 1940s both countries used all kinds of animals, including fruit flies, mice, hamsters, guinea pigs, cats, dogs, rabbits, frogs, goldfish, monkeys and even worms, to test their reactions to the potential effects of travelling in space. The vast majority of these animals died during the research procedures.

In July 1951 the Soviet Union sent two dogs into space and they became the first living higher animals to be successfully recovered from a spaceflight, and in November 1957 the Soviets sent Laika,

Mercury-Redstone 2 launch with Ham aboard.

the first dog and first living creature to orbit the Earth and which, it is now believed, died from overheating and panic just a few hours after the mission started.

The US sent a squirrel monkey into space which died when the nose cone recovery parachute failed to operate; then eventually two rhesus monkeys became the first primates to survive space flight.

But scientists were still nervous of sending a human into space, so decided to use the next best thing: chimps, our closest relative. The position of their internal organs and skeletal suspension are similar to ours[1], so chimps were considered ideal to test a spacecraft's life-support system.

So they used young chimps captured in the French Cameroons in West Africa; this inevitably involved killing their mothers and decimating the chimps' social groups.

Initially these young chimps were used as crash-test dummies, spun at high speed in centrifuges, squeezed in compression chambers and subjected to zero gravity and sleep deprivation. Most of these chimps died because of equipment failures.

In a test codenamed Project Whoosh in July 1955, chimps strapped in an open seat were ejected from Cherokee missiles at an altitude of about five miles. On its website NASA (National Aeronautics and Space Administration) says: "This project was not a total loss" since "the failures were instructive".

NASA was formed in October 1958 when Eisenhower was US president, but it was his successor, President Kennedy, who had real enthusiasm for the space programme, which he said would be among his administration's most important legacies.

In April 1959 NASA launched Project Mercury and though they called this their "man-in-space program" a more accurate description would have been their "chimps-in-space program".

Ham

Ham was the United States' first active astronaut, albeit a great ape. Chimps had previously travelled as passive passengers, but Ham performed complicated tasks while in space.

It is believed that Ham was born in July 1957 and was among those captured in the French Cameroons. One of a group of chimps, he was taken to Rare Bird Farm in Miami, Florida, then bought by the United States Air Force and brought to NASA's Holloman Air Force Base in New Mexico in 1959. Ham's name was an acronym of the laboratory which prepared him for his historic mission – the Holloman Aerospace Medical Center. Some think the name also honoured the commander of the laboratory, Lt Col Hamilton Blackshear.

Ham was known as 'primate No 65' before his flight, and was only renamed Ham upon his successful return to earth. It is likely that this was to avoid any bad press that would result from the death of a 'named' chimpanzee if the mission were a failure[2]. Ham was only three when he was sent into space, an age when in natural circumstances he would still have been inseparable from his mother.

There were originally 40 chimps being considered for space flight but after some tests they were reduced to 18, then to six, including Ham and Enos, also bought from Rare Bird Farm. It is believed that the rejected chimps were sold on for medical research.

While the chimps were being trained, each individual was assigned to a member of the NASA team and most of these men became fond of their charges. Ed Dittmer was the trainer and handler for Ham and Enos.

Two groups

The chimps were separated into two groups in different compounds as a precaution against the spread of diseases. Mercury capsule mock-ups were installed in both, and the chimps worked

Ham with a technician 'inspecting' the equipment, including his miniature space suit, in preparation for his launch.

45

daily at their 'psychomotor' performance tasks. To prepare them for space they were first trained to do simple, timed tasks in response to electric lights and sounds, while restrained in a seat beneath three lights with corresponding levers. They were taught to push a lever within five seconds of seeing a flashing blue light; failure to do so resulted in a mild electric shock to the soles of their feet, while a correct response earned them a banana pellet. Chimps' skin is much tougher than ours, so these shocks probably didn't cause too much distress.

All six chimps were treated as possible 'astronauts' until the day before the flight, when each was given a physical examination then rated according to data received from sensors, tests on their reflexes and their responses to the lights and levers. The chosen chimp would need to be able to carry out all the learned tests during weightlessness and re-entry into the earth's atmosphere.

Ham was described as a 'smart, lovable chimp' with a good temperament, and his positive personality was given as one of the main reasons he was chosen for flight. During his training Ham had a back-up called Mini. When she was no longer needed, she became part of an Air Force chimpanzee breeding programme. She had nine babies and helped to raise the young of other chimps at the base. She survived all the other space chimps and died in March 1998 aged 41.

Lift off

Ham's space journey took place on January 31st 1961 from the Kennedy Space Center at Cape Canaveral, Florida. He was dressed in a miniature space suit over a nappy and rubber pants, then fitted into a biopack couch to keep him still. This was secured into the Mercury-Redstone 2 capsule at 7.53 am. Lift off was four hours later – a long wait for a confused, restrained young chimp.

Ham, aged about three, posing with a carer for the camera at Cape Canaveral, illustrating just how young he was for the task ahead of him.

While he was in space Ham successfully pushed the lever as he had been trained to do and his activities and tasks were monitored, using computers back on Earth. They showed that his performance was less than a second slower than during training, demonstrating that tasks could indeed be performed successfully in space. The capsule suffered a partial loss of pressure during the flight, but it was said that Ham's spacesuit prevented him from suffering any harm. He experienced a total of 6.6 minutes of weightlessness.

Capsized on impact

The capsule reached an altitude of 127 miles and a speed of 5,857 mph and the flight lasted 16 minutes, 39 seconds, travelling 422 miles before it splashed down at 12.12pm in the Atlantic Ocean. But it capsized on impact; 800 lbs of seawater leaked into Ham's capsule through two holes in the titanium pressure bulkhead. Ham was in the water, literally, for nearly three hours before he was rescued at 2.52pm. A search plane had sighted the floating capsule and the Navy dispatched helicopters from a nearby ship.

Ham suffered a bruised nose during the landing, and a medical examination found him to be slightly fatigued and dehydrated, but otherwise he was said to be in good condition physically. Observers said Ham must have enjoyed his trip, as he was grinning, but a chimp's grin is a sign of fear (an open mouth with lips covering the teeth denotes happiness). An indication of how Ham really felt can be guessed from the fact that when the press later wanted to take photos of him in his space couch he fought against being strapped in again.

Ham's mission led directly to the successful launch of America's

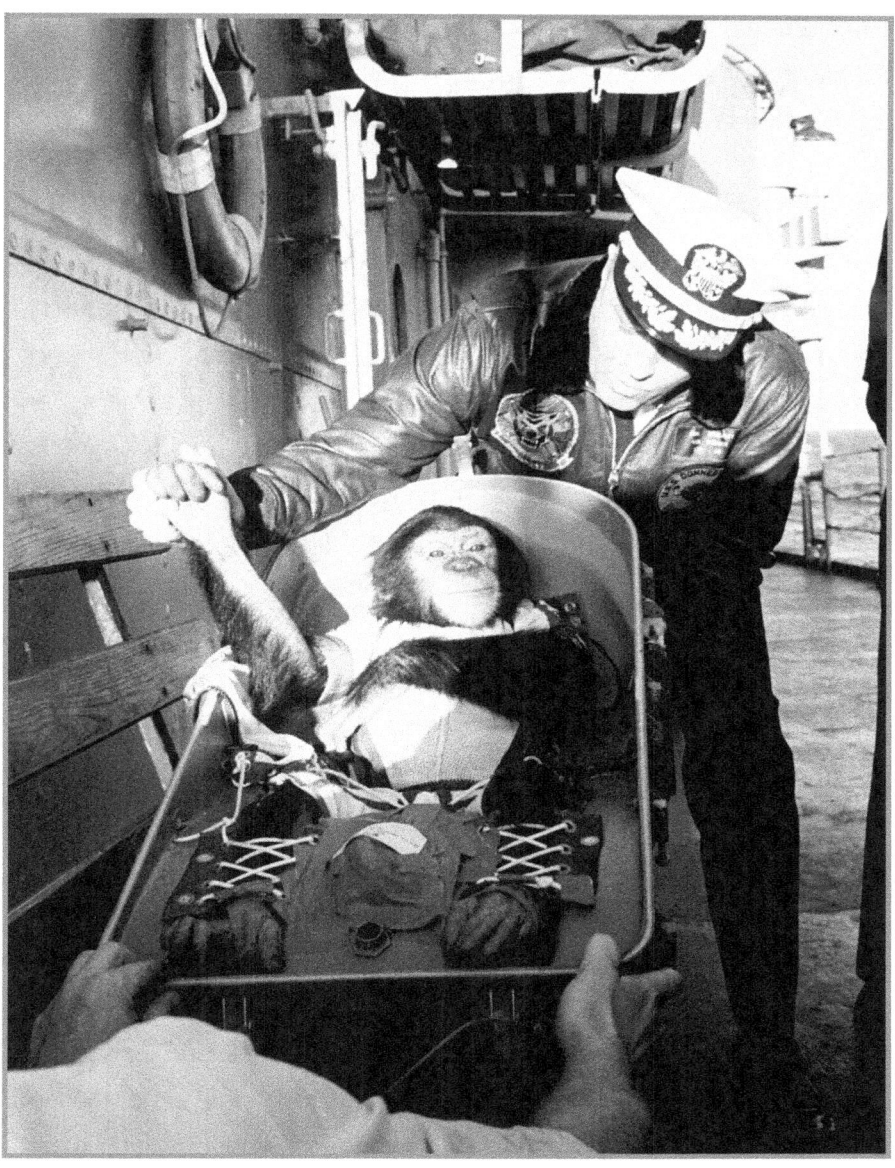

Ham is greeted by the commander of the recovery ship after his flight on the Mercury Redstone rocket. This became known as the "hand shake" welcome.

PHOTO COURTESY OF NASA

first human astronaut, Alan B. Shepard Jr, on May 5th, 1961[3], aboard the Mercury-Redstone 3 Freedom 7 spacecraft – a flight which carried him to an altitude of 116 miles.

Back on earth

Ham was retained by the US Air Force until 1963 when he was sent to the National Zoological Park in Washington, DC. For a while he was treated as a celebrity and was a popular attraction. His photo was chosen for the cover of *Life Magazine*, and he appeared several times on television, in newsreels and in a film with Evel Knievel. But because of his intensive training, lack of chimp social skills and a earlier life with only humans for company, he was unable to make friends with other chimps. The zoo attempted to find Ham a mate but he couldn't relate to his own kind.

In the early 1980s he was transferred to the North Carolina State Zoo where he was introduced more sensitively to other chimps with some success. But in January 1983 Ham died at the age of 27, two years after joining the zoo and just as he was beginning to settle and enjoy other chimps' company.

Even then Ham wasn't left in peace. There was some discussion about what to do with his remains and it was even suggested he be stuffed and put on display. But this didn't happen and the Armed Forces Institute of Pathology kept his skeleton for research purposes, and the remainder of his body was laid to rest in grounds at the front of the International Space Hall of Fame in Alamogordo, New Mexico.

Enos

Enos (Greek for 'man') was destined for a longer and riskier trip than Ham. Following on from their success with Shepard, the US was now keen to send an astronaut into orbit. Enos was chosen for the dummy run; he was five years old and described as temperamental and less compliant than Ham. One observer, comparing photos of both chimps constrained in their couches, commented that Ham's arms were not bound but Enos' usually were.

Enos received 1,263 hours of training over a 16-month period, including 343 hours under restraint. The testing equipment was more complicated than Ham's had been. Enos was given a four-problem cycle to complete, consisting of tests lasting 12 minutes separated by six minutes of rest, which would be continuous during his space mission.

One test presented right and left hand levers which Enos could use to turn off lights, avoiding a mild shock to the left foot. (An observer commented that one chimp pulled levers 7,000 times in 70 minutes, making only 28 errors.)

Another was a delayed response experiment: 20 seconds after a green light appeared on the panel, Enos needed to press a lever to receive a drink of water. Although there was no penalty for his failure to respond, if he pulled the lever too early he received nothing and the problem was presented again.

A further test involved pulling a lever exactly 50 times to receive a banana pellet; this was also voluntary and without a penalty. A NASA spokesman said: "The intelligence of these chimpanzees was remarkable. More or less than 50 pulls caused the training unit to recycle without giving any reward." An observer said that the chimps in training would pull the lever "bangity-bangity-bang" about 45 times, then carefully pull numbers 46, 47, 48, and 49, and finally number 50 with one hand cupped under the dispenser to receive the reward.

Fruit machine

In another test, three symbols – circles, triangles, and squares - appeared in various combinations, like a fruit machine, and Enos had to pull a lever under the symbol which was the odd one out. If he got this wrong he received a mild shock. (It's interesting to note that a chimp is clever enough to recognise circles, triangles and squares having never done a geometry lesson! [4]) Enos' lack of response during rest periods was deemed to indicate that he was well oriented to a spacecraft environment.

On November 29th 1961 a Mercury-Atlas rocket with Enos strapped inside was launched from Cape Canaveral; the aim was to complete three orbits, but due to technical difficulties the flight terminated after two. The malfunction caused Enos some suffering; for every correct move he made he was given a shock instead of a banana pellet. Despite this discomfort, Enos continued to make the correct moves. His capsule splashed down in the recovery area in the Atlantic after a flight of 3 hours, 20 minutes and 59 seconds. He had flown 50,892 miles.

The capsule was spotted by a search plane and the nearest ship hauled Enos' capsule aboard 1 hour and 15 minutes after it landed. Enos was said to be in good overall condition.

Enos' mission, despite the malfunctions, was deemed successful enough to press ahead with John Glenn's orbit of the earth in Mercury-Atlas 6 on February 20th 1962. Glenn was the first human to orbit the earth and the third American in space (the second had been Virgil Grissom on a suborbital flight in July 1961).

Enos died at Holloman Air Force Base of dysentery 11 months after his flight. An ignominious end for a heroic and clever space traveller.

Afterwards

In the early 1970s, the US Air Force announced that it no longer needed chimps for research; they were described by the USAF in a *Wall Street Journal* article as "surplus equipment". But this didn't mean the chimps could be retired. First they were leased out for biomedical research, then in 1997 were sold to a laboratory at the Coulston Foundation in Alamogordo, New Mexico.

This unhappy situation came to the attention of Dr Carole Noon, a biological anthropologist and lifelong champion of animal rights. With the financial assistance of the Arcus Foundation, she founded the Save the Chimps charity the same year in an attempt to rescue chimps from the Coulston Foundation. According to the charity the Foundation had "the worst record of any lab in the history of the Animal Welfare Act".

On site were more than 140 veterans or descendants of chimps used in the early days of space research. Dr Noon sued the Air Force on the chimps' behalf and, after a year-long struggle, settled out of court for custody of just 21 chimps.

In 2002 the Coulston Foundation was declared bankrupt, giving Dr Noon the opportunity she had been waiting for. With a grant from the Arcus Foundation and the backing of veteran primatologist, Jane Goodall and clinical psychologist and expert on chimpanzees, Dr Roger Fouts (see chapter on Washoe and Nim on p13), Dr Noon purchased the Alamogordo laboratory and rescued 266 chimps and 61 monkeys. The result was the creation of the world's largest chimpanzee sanctuary at Save The Chimps.

Dr Noon made it her life's work to improve the chimps' conditions, train staff to care for them, raise funds for their care and introduce the chimps into 'families' before they were relocated to their new home, a permanent rescue sanctuary on the 150-acre Fort Pierce in Florida.

Four laps

Dr Noon died of cancer in May 2009, aged 59, but she had lived long enough to see 159 of her rescued chimps transported 2,000 miles to the sanctuary, travelling ten at a time in a specially adapted trailer. They had all arrived by late 2011, and it was estimated that their rescue vehicle had travelled a distance equivalent to four laps of the Earth – a fitting statistic for the space chimps.

Save The Chimps is a non profit organisation and claims to have the largest chimp population in the world. At time of writing there were 254 chimps living there, though the sanctuary has cared for more.

Among the former space chimps were Lil Mini, Mini's daughter; Dana, who had survived research in the 1960s; Marty, who had taken part in a 'data acquisition flight' in 1965; Gogi, who had been used to study the effects of rapid decompression; and Gromek, whose blood had been used in tests. When he arrived at the sanctuary in 2000, it was the first time the chimp had been out of a cage in nearly 40 years.

The sanctuary is spread over 200 acres divided into a dozen 3.5-acre islands. The water surrounding each island acts as a natural barrier – chimps don't like water. The only fencing is around the buildings where they sleep and feed. No members of the public are allowed in and staff are not allowed to touch them. The chimps live in family groups of about 25 to each island, where they are free to roam in enclosures, run free in the grass, climb on jungle gyms and laze in hammocks.

Sanctuary director, Jen Feuerstein said: "It's really exciting and emotional for the chimps when they go out onto the island for the first time. Often they will hug and kiss one another as if to say, 'Look at this, it's all for us'."

Their former diet consisted of monkey chow, similar to dog biscuits. Now they have fresh fruit and vegetables, plus treats such as sunflower seeds hidden inside tennis balls, and bamboo filled with peanut butter. Lists on the kitchen walls note the daily menu, and indicate any chimps with food allergies.

The sanctuary relies solely on charity to support the chimps; they say that NASA and the US government have never donated any money, unlike the human astronauts, including Bob Crippen, who have helped out financially.

Feuerstein said: "Chimps are remarkably forgiving. If I had been in their position, I think I would probably hate the entire human race – but they don't. They warm quickly to people who treat them with friendliness and compassion. That's all they ask."

She added: "When the astronauts came back from their space missions they received ticker-tape parades and were rightfully considered heroes. But the chimps were forgotten and relegated along with their descendants to biomedical research laboratories.

"Now that we have become a lot more familiar with space we know in retrospect: 'Hey, we could have put someone up there without all these tests', but that's hindsight. Back in the Fifties and Sixties we really didn't know a lot about chimps, and there probably weren't a lot of alternatives to test spaceflight and reach this lofty goal of going to the Moon. These chimps were captured from their forest homes and transplanted to a life of captivity, fear and pain."

Astronauts visit

In May 2009, to celebrate the 40th anniversary of the Moon shot, the chimps received a well-publicised visit from astronauts Scott Carpenter and Bob Crippen, accompanied by reporters and camera crews. Carpenter was the second American to orbit the Earth, and Crippen piloted Columbia on the first space shuttle flight in 1981.

The men said that they felt the visit to the sanctuary was appropriate as they and the chimps had all been involved in the same space projects. As the two astronauts drove around the sanctuary, staff members pointed out each chimp by name.

Carpenter said that he wasn't sure that the chimps had proved space flight safe for humans, because even a young chimp is many times stronger than an adult human male: "They're capable of withstanding a lot more stress than people are." But he added: "It gave us the resolve to press on. From one retired space traveller to another, I appreciate their contributions to space exploration. We're paying them back for their service."

Crippen commented: "There were a lot of unknowns back in the '50s about how the human body would react to space, and some real concerns that you might die. [The chimps] opened that up to give people confidence that it was OK to put Al Shepard and the guys up for the first time. These guys [the chimps] contributed a lot to where we are at now from a technical standpoint and a scientific standpoint. It's really nice to give them a nice place to retire."

Buzz Aldrin has also commented on the chimps' role in space travel. He said that the astronauts appreciated "the enormous debt we owe the space chimpanzees. They and their descendants have served us in so many ways – initially as substitute humans in space

---

Endangered species

IN September 2015 the United States Fish and Wildlife Service (USFWS) declared that all chimpanzees were an endangered species, including captive chimpanzees in the US.

The organisation had already deemed wild chimpanzees to be endangered in 1990, but captive chimpanzees had been listed as "threatened", denying them the protection afforded by the Endangered Species Act. Save The Chimps statec: "This so-called 'split listing' has come to an end. Extending the endangered species designation to captive chimpanzees makes it highly unlikely that laboratories will continue to do medical experimentation upon chimpanzees. Also it will be more difficult to use chimpanzees in the entertainment industry and the pet trade."

At this date there were almost 1,000 captive chimpanzees living in non-sanctuary settings throughout the US.

research. Now it is time to repay this debt by giving these veterans the peaceful and permanent retirement they deserve."

And a last word from NASA: "Over the past 50 years, American and Soviet scientists have utilised the animal world for testing. Despite losses, these animals have taught the scientists a tremendous amount more than could have been learned without them. Without animal testing in the early days of the human space programme, the Soviet and American programmes could have suffered great losses of human life. These animals performed a service to their respective countries that no human could or would have performed. They gave their lives and/or their service in the name of technological advancement, paving the way for humanity's many forays into space."

It's doubtful whether Ham, Enos and their chimp peers would have given their consent though, if they'd been asked.

[1] (p43) A study in April 2015 published in BMC Evolutionary Biology found that people with lower back problems are more likely to have a spine similar in shape to the chimpanzee. The findings showed that the vertebrae of humans with disc problems are closer in shape to those of the chimpanzee than are the vertebrae of humans without disc problems. The study suggested that over many thousands of years humans have not all adapted in the same way and that the pathological vertebrae of some people may be less well adapted for walking upright.

[2] (p44) Primatologist, Jane Goodall said that while studying at Cambridge she was told: "I shouldn't have named the chimps and that they should have had numbers. I wasn't allowed to talk about them having personalities, and certainly not about them thinking or having emotions. But then I thought back to my childhood teacher who taught me that this wasn't true – my dog."

[3] (p50) Shepard was just beaten by Yuri Gagarin of The Soviet Union who became

the first human in space aboard a Vostok spacecraft which completed an orbit of the Earth on April 12th 1961.

[4] (p52) In her book *Through A Window*, Jane Goodall points out that chimps have pre-mathematical skills: "They can readily differentiate between 'more' and 'less'... they have no difficulty in separating a pile of food into 'fruits' and 'vegetables' [then] dividing the same pile of food into 'large' versus 'small' items, even though this requires putting some vegetables with some fruit." (Also see 'Number crunching chimps' on page 87.)

"Researchers find it very necessary to keep blinkers on. They don't want to admit that the animals they are working with have feelings. They don't want to admit that they might have minds and personalities because that would make it quite difficult for them to do what they do; so we find that within the lab communities there is a very strong resistance among the researchers to admitting that animals have minds, personalities and feelings."

Jane Goodall

Chimps' tea parties

YOUNG chimps at London Zoo found it easy and enjoyable playing with tea-time props and 'misbehaving' at the right moment, but because they were chimps, not humans, they had no sense of being exploited or of entrapment.

From the 1920s to the early 1970s London Zoo staged a popular regular summer event which "challenged neither its audience nor its performers"[1] and which became hugely popular and a great draw for visitors. Young chimps, dressed in smart clothes to look like humans, were led out by their keepers to an enclosed area where a table was set for tea. The chimps sat down and were given food and drink as if they were people.

The chimps poured out drinks from teapots, often missing the cups, then tucked in to the treats laid out on the table. The keepers would pretend to 'scold' them if they 'misbehaved', but inevitably the spectacle would disintegrate, with chimps throwing food and drink around and getting down from the table and running around. It was their lack of 'manners' which made the event so humorous – and so popular, especially with children.

The riotous tea times attracted huge numbers of visitors to the zoo, willing to pay a small fee to see the chimps behaving like humans out of control, but there was also a serious side to the chimp-style fun and games: the zoo authorities believed that these chaotic events could help them learn about primate behaviour.

Although it was probably not apparent to the audience, all the tea party chimps were juveniles, as is the case with the vast majority of performing apes; adult chimps were generally too strong and independent to be reliable performers.

Lucrative business

But where did these young chimps come from? What had happened to their mothers? We know that during the early part of the 20th century hunters travelled to countries inhabited by great apes, shooting adult females and taking their babies; this was a lucrative business as zoos worldwide were eager to buy the captive apes to increase visitor numbers. Unlike other exotic species, most of the hunted young chimps survived the trauma of capture and restraint. They were stronger than the humans they so closely resembled and could be nourished with bottle feeding, a relatively easy procedure compared to that required for other transported exotic animals. So zoos were able to fill their cages with chimps and the tea parties became a common feature throughout the world.

Travelling fairs had entertained audiences using trained apes and monkeys from about the beginning of the 18th century and tea parties for chimps are thought to date back to the mid-nineteenth century and possibly earlier, though there is not much archive evidence to substantiate this. There is a photograph of a 1911 tea party at the Bronx Zoo in New York where two young chimps and three young orangutans are sitting around a table covered with a tablecloth, four of them in high chairs. A uniformed keeper presides over them and the apes appear to be enjoying whatever they are drinking. Orangutans have rarely been used for this kind of entertainment, as they are not so demonstrative nor so gregarious as chimps.

London Zoo exhibited chimps as early as 1883 but tea parties did not begin there until 1926. (In 1935 a Pets' Corner was established, becoming a Children's Zoo in 1938.)

Television shows

Zoologist and author, Desmond Morris was director of London Zoo in the middle of the 20th century when he also presented popular television shows featuring animals, including chimps. He commented

Chimps taking part in a London Zoo tea party in 1970.

PHOTO BY GARWOOD/ANL/REX SHUTTERSTOCK

that the tea party chimps were actively encouraged to play the fool and by doing so demonstrated how intelligent they were.

He said: "Each afternoon at a set time a group of young chimpanzees performed at a table for the amusement of zoo visitors. They were trained to use bowls, plates, spoons, cups and a teapot. For the chimpanzee brain, learning to perform these trivial tasks provided only a minor challenge. There was the ever present danger that their table manners would become too polished. In order to relieve the monotony, it often became necessary to train them to "misbehave". They excelled at this too and their timing became so perfect that the tea cups were always popped into the teapot and the tea drunk from the spout, just at the vital moment when the keeper turned his back."

Allen, Park and Wat, authors of *Anthropomorphism, Orientalism and Colonialism* (1994) said they believed that the popularity and persistence of the chimps' tea parties "cannot be explained by saying simply that it was amusing, although that was no doubt a factor. Instead, a chimpanzee tea party presented to its audience a constellation of incongruities: animal/human, child/adult, proscribed [to forbid or ban] behaviour/prescribed behaviour, wild/tame, improvisation/scripted performance. Although simple in execution, the chimp tea party was a complex entertainment."

Foreign zoos

During the 1950s London Zoo also trained chimps for use in foreign zoos; they were sent as far away as Moscow and New Zealand. It is not known what became of the Moscow emigrants, but some of the New Zealand chimps were reported as being still alive during the

1990s. Because they were hand-reared by humans and didn't learn to socialise they found it hard to relate to their own kind, in common with other captive chimps. They were kept segregated from the more "natural" chimps, who were able to enjoy an open enclosure. In fact, the tea party chimps were said not to have been fond of open spaces and were happier in cage-like quarters.

Undignified

By the end of the 1960s the supply of wild-caught young chimps was diminishing, public taste was changing and it was becoming politically incorrect and undignified to make chimps perform as proto-human clowns. And television technology was advancing, and viewers now preferred to watch unfettered apes filmed in their natural habitat rather than their captive cousins being forced to behave like bad-mannered people.

At the same time the zoo keeper, who had acted as a human 'mediator' between the audience and the chimps at the tea parties, was being replaced on the small screen by someone with more input, a scientist or knowledgeable presenter. The London Zoo chimp tea parties came to an end in 1972.

Zoos were also coming under pressure from animal rights campaigners to give their animals more space, and the chimps, along with other animals, were moved out of small restricting cages into larger enclosures where they had room to climb and run around in a more natural environment.

However, the fact that the public could no longer see so many animals up close, combined with advances in filming them in the wild for television programmes, meant that zoos began to lose their popularity. They now tend to emphasise education and animal conservation rather than entertainment, and some have become theme parks to ensure the visitors keep coming.

[1] (p60) *Anthropomorphism, Orientalism and Colonialism*, Allen, Park and Wat (1994)

"Just imagine taking some normal people, stripping off their clothes, taking away all their other possessions, depriving them of the power of speech, and reducing them to grunting, without changing their anatomy at all. Put them in a cage in the zoo next to the chimp cages, and let the rest of us clothed and talking people visit the zoo. Those speechless caged people would be seen for what we all really are: a chimp that has little hair and walks upright. A zoologist from outer space would immediately classify us as just a third species of chimpanzee, along with the pygmy chimp of Zaire and the common chimp of the rest of tropical Africa."

Jared Diamond, *The rise and fall of the third chimpanzee*

PG Tips chimps

HOW Mother and Monkey saved chimps from being exploited in the pursuit of profit and commercial success.

In 1956, while the chimps' tea parties at London Zoo were still delighting the visitors, advertising agency, Davidson Pearce Berry and Spottiswoode, were asked by UK tea distributors Brooke Bond to come up with a good idea to advertise its PG Tips brand. They produced a TV commercial featuring four chimps taking part in a 'tea party' with a voice-over by actor Peter Sellers – a spoof on the zoo's popular event. The result was *Stately Home* which was aired in the UK on Christmas Day that year. Viewers loved it and the chimp-centred advertising campaign became one of the longest and most successful ever in Britain. Within two years, PG Tips had risen from fourth in the market to become Britain's top-selling tea, thanks to a group of performing chimps.

Tony Toller, advertising writer for the agency at the time, said: "The chimps were the heroes rather than the product. They hit people in the face. They thought: 'This is amazing. These aren't humans. These aren't actors. They're chimpanzees.'"[1]

During the late 1950s the chimps were mostly borrowed from Billy Smart's Circus, then from 1960 they were provided by carers Molly Badham and Natalie Evans (see page 70). The young chimps were dressed up and trained to 'act out' short scenes. 'Secretary' chimps in curly wigs served tea to 'company directors', chimp cyclists took part in a *Tour de France* spoof and in *Mr Shifter* a 'moving man' and his 'apprentice' struggled to move a piano downstairs; this popular advert was broadcast 1,900 times altogether. Many of the adverts featured the voices of celebrities, including Bob Monkhouse and Cilla Black.

Humorous though these adverts were, they involved training chimps to perform actions they wouldn't naturally do. And, like the London Zoo tea party entertainers, only young chimps were used for 'acting' before they became too large and aggressive.

In the early 1960s (when Britons were drinking 73 billion cups of tea a year) the ad agency gave the chimps more pronounced human personalities. They produced an advert featuring a 'cowboy' wearing a stetson and carrying a six-gun, who was greeted by a 'bartender' with the phrase: "Want a drinky, stranger?" According to Toller, It became a national catchphrase and was "quoted a hell of a lot".

In the late 1960s, as London Zoo's chimp tea parties were beginning to lose their popularity and the public's view of performing chimps was changing, Brooke Bond temporarily stopped using chimps for their TV advertising.

As a result, sales of PG Tips dropped sharply. Toller said the company wrongly thought the chimp ads "were in danger of becoming boring. How wrong they were."

So adverts using chimps were brought back after 18 months, despite growing criticism from animal rights activists as well as the general public, of using trained apes for entertainment and profit.

The chimps were finally replaced in 2002 with four 'claymation' flatmates called the T-Birds, loosely based on the television series *Friends* and created by Aardman Animations, makers of the *Wallace and Gromit* films. But the T-Birds didn't catch on with the public in the same way as the chimps.

Unilever bought the PG Tips brand from Brooke Bond in 1984 and appointed a new advertising agency, Mother. The team at Mother was mindful of the fact that the chimps had been popular, but acknowledged that they could no longer use real ones. So they came up with a fresh idea for the TV adverts in 2007, this time using a knitted 'chimp' called Monkey. He had originally appeared in adverts for the failed ITV Digital company alongside Johnny Vegas[2]. Monkey and Vegas once again starred together in the new tea adverts and were an instant hit, Ben Miller providing Monkey's 'voice'. The grey and green woollen character became hugely popular and featured on all kinds of PG tips merchandising.

Mother's creative director, Darren Bailes, said: "When developing the campaign we sat through almost 50 years worth of PG Tips chimps adverts, and it was amazing how fresh and relevant much still felt and how closely they reflected contemporary life and humour."

He said that *Tour de France* captured the nation's obsession with all things cycling-related and *Mr Shifter* coincided with the peak in popularity of the television series *Steptoe and Son* (in the advert an 'apprentice' asks his 'dad' if he knows the piano is on his foot to which his 'dad' replies: "You hum it, son, I'll play it").

Well-earned retirement

The original PG Tips chimps were taken to Twycross Zoo, Leicestershire (see page 70), where a remaining elderly contingent

The grey and green woollen character rapidly became popular and appeared on various PG tips merchandising.

are enjoying a well-earned retirement. Louis, who had 'starred' as James Bond in adverts during the 1970s and 1980s, died in 2013 aged 37, after a short illness. Twycross curator and head of life sciences, Dr Charlotte Macdonald, said: "Louis was a very gentle and laid-back chimp – a favourite with everyone."

Hero women

From 1960 most of the chimps used in the PG Tips adverts were the responsibility of two remarkable women living in the village of Hints in Staffordshire, UK, who eventually set up and ran Twycross Zoo in Leicestershire.

Molly Badham and Natalie Evans initially ran rival pet shops in the village, then became friends and joined forces. They became aware of the plight of young chimps which were being bought as pets, then either died through neglect, were abandoned or given to laboratories when they grew too big to handle. The problem was becoming acute; the London Zoo tea parties were giving the impression that chimps were like cute humans, and at this time there were no restrictions on shops selling exotic animals, including chimps; they could even be bought at Harrods.

Badham's niece, Jane Storkey[1], said the two women took in all kinds of animals from people who couldn't manage them, but chimps were their favourites.

A total of 15 young chimps were reared by Badham and Evans over a period of 20 years; all were originally orphans from Africa. Badham had been a dog trainer and used this knowledge when handling the chimps. Storkey said Badham had a special knack. If a chimp dropped a banana skin on the kitchen floor, she would tell him to pick it up and put it in the bin and he would obey. "She was like the chimp whisperer, she could make them do exactly what they were told."

Storkey grew up in the 1950s across the road from the zoo that her aunt ran. She said she would play with one of the chimps on a see-saw or they would ride bikes together. Evans would make both girl and chimp cups of tea and jam sandwiches.

"Whenever I went into their kitchen, there would be two or three chimps sitting up at the table, very well behaved, much better brought up in fact than some of my schoolfriends. Sam [the chimp] was my best friend. Even when we grew up and he lived to be 40 I

Molly Badham and one of her chimps.

would visit him and he always knew exactly who I was."

Dorothy Phillips, a former keeper at Twycross Zoo, said: "Their method of chimp rearing was eccentric. They brought them up as children; they dressed them in sensible clothes and gave them a healthy and varied diet with treats like cake and orange juice. They took them for walks in the local woods to get exercise and fresh air. They let Sue the oldest chimp have an occasional smoke.

"The chimps were quick to pick things up. If they saw you eat with a spoon they'd have a go."

Deal was struck

The two women became well known for their chimp expertise and in 1960 they received a phone call from Brooke Bond asking if the chimps could be used as actors in the PG Tips adverts. The deal was struck. Each new campaign pushed the chimps further and they needed daily training sessions. What used to be essentially a hobby for Badham and Evans now became hard work.

The chimps were earning for their owners £100 a week at their peak in the early 1960s, the equivalent of about £100,000 a year today. The women used the income to launch their own zoo on 12 acres of land near the village of Twycross, Leicestershire, now a primate breeding centre.

The zoo opened in May 1963 and was an immediate success. There were often queues to see the chimps who had 'acted' in the adverts. Badham and Evans organised a daily extravaganza with chimps on bicycles, stilts and scooters. And they were still financed by Brooke Bond. Then in 1968 the company told them that the chimps were being made redundant. However, after 18 months of decreasing tea sales for Brooke Bond and loss of earnings for Badham and Evans the chimps were reinstated.

The agency now decided that the chimps should behave even more like humans and wanted them to lipsynch exactly with the dialogue.

Storkey said that Badham taught the chimps to talk on command. She would point and whisper "Talk" and the animals would click their teeth and smack their lips. This would be matched to the voiceover dialogue. The adverts became even more ambitious, with the trainers encouraging the chimps to ride bikes while following a moving camera. But the chimps got bored easily and this resulted in many more takes than there would have been for human actors. But the effort was worth it; PG Tips became top tea brand once more. The adverts were so popular that customers were demanding 'monkey tea' when they went shopping.

Brooke Bond organised chimp road shows so the public could meet their heroes and the chimps were in demand for celebrity appearances such as cutting ribbons at supermarket openings. Badham and Evans accompanied their chimps all over country.

By the late 1970s the ad agency was asking Badham to teach the chimps increasingly complicated tricks and she objected to the chimps being pushed too far. So the Twycross chimps were dropped and the agency hired a troupe of Italian chimps instead who had been trained to roller-skate and perform ballet moves. They also used chimps from New York who'd been taught to 'type'.

Toller commented: "The pressure to innovate was enormous."

But the foreign replacements didn't have the charm of their British predecessors and weren't so popular with the viewing public.

Natural environment

Documentaries were beginning to be shown on television about wild animals, including chimps, in their natural environment, and this gave Badham the good intention of sending some of her chimps to Africa to be reintroduced to their natural environment.

Dorothy Phillips was given the responsibility. In 1975 she flew with one male and two female chimps to Dacha, then they undertook a 300 mile journey to base camp. But the project was a disaster; one chimp died of exhaustion and as soon as the other two were released they ran away into the bush in panic. Phillips said she wandered for days looking for them, then found one dead. The Twycross women never tried to release chimps into the wild again.

The zoo managed to remain self-supporting, still using the Brooke Bond association, and Badham wrote a biography called *Chimps with everything*. She spent the rest of her life looking after her now ageing chimps. She died in 2007.

The present day Twycross encourages chimps to live as natural a life as possible. At time of writing a PG Tips female chimp called Choppers was still surviving at the age of 46. She was six weeks old when her mother was killed by poachers in Sierra Leone.

Diane Locke[1], an aid worker from Gabon, Africa said: "She was tiny with no teeth, traumatised, in shock and injured in an elbow and a knee. It was like being handed a human baby. I could hold her in the palm of my hand.

"Even though part of you said you shouldn't have wild animals, what could you do? When something had its arms around your neck you found it difficult to put it down."

Locke looked after Choppers until she was four, then when she left Africa she felt she could neither leave the chimp behind nor take her home with her. She said: "She had no bush skills and would have been dead within a week."

Locke found out about Badham and Evans' refuge and took her there. A 2014 Channel 5 film *Secrets of the Tea Chimps* (see note below) shows Choppers being reunited with Locke, the chimp recognising and greeting her former carer.

[1] (pp66, 70 and 74) Quotes from Storkey and Toller and information about Badham and Evans are taken from a Channel 5 documentary in 2014 called *Secrets of the Tea Chimps*, and information is also taken from a 2014 *Daily Mail* feature by Christopher Steven.

[2] (p68) ITV Digital was a British digital terrestrial television broadcaster, which offered a pay-TV service on the world's first digital terrestrial television network. Initially launched as ONdigital in 1998, the service was re-branded as ITV Digital in July 2001. Low audience take-up and a mis-judged multi-million pound deal with the Football League led to massive losses and ITV Digital was forced into administration in March 2002. Despite the demise of the company, its advertising icon Monkey was a resounding hit. As an incentive customers who signed up to the service had been sent a knitted version and when the company ceased trading people paid large sums to obtain secondhand Monkeys.

"Some folks seem to have descended from the chimpanzee much later than others..."

Kin Hubbard

Clever chimps

USING chimps as subjects for experimental research has its detractors, but closely observing our ape cousins in as natural environment as possible, whether in African reservations or European sanctuaries, makes it possible to determine just how intelligent and remarkable they are, in some cases outperforming their human cousins. Here are some insights into the chimp mind.

Problem-solving chimps

SCIENTISTS were studying chimps' intelligence and behaviour as early as the beginning of the twentieth century.

A German psychologist, Wolfgang Köhler, wrote *The Mentality of Apes* in 1917 in which he explained that he was inspired to work with chimpanzees because the "structure of their brains is more closely related to the chemistry of the human body and brain-structure than to the chemical nature of the lower apes and their brain development". He was intrigued that human traits could be observed in the everyday behaviour of chimpanzees.

Köhler was fascinated to see how chimpanzees solve problems. When bananas were positioned out of reach they stacked wooden crates to use as makeshift ladders, in order to access them. When the fruit was placed on the ground outside their cage they used sticks to extend the reach of their arms. Köhler concluded that the chimps had not arrived at these methods through trial-and-error (which other psychologists had claimed), but rather that having come up with a solution to the problem, they proceeded to carry it out in a way that was, in Köhler's words, "unwaveringly purposeful". Köhler's work on the mentality of apes was seen as a turning point in the psychology of thinking.

The following reports are from the BBC website:

Five dimensional chimps

CHIMPS not only have individual personalities but they have ones similar to humans, according to a study published in the journal *Animal Behaviour* in 2013.

Dr Alexander Weiss, senior lecturer at the University of Edinburgh, said that human personality is categorised into five 'dimensions', sometimes known as 'the big five': neuroticism, extroversion, openness to experience, agreeableness and conscientiousness.

Previous studies into non-human primates suggested that chimpanzees shared these five dimensions with humans, whilst orangutans, though similar to humans in many ways, display only three of the five: extraversion, neuroticism and agreeableness.

These shared personality dimensions are not surprising considering our genetic similarities, said Weiss: "Humans and chimps shared a common ancestor about six to eight million years ago." The common ancestor for humans and orangutans is thought to have existed as far back as 15 million years ago, which explains why chimpanzees and humans are likely to be more similar in personality (see 'Neither ape nor human' on page 94).

Mark Adams, who helped carry out the research while studying for his PhD at the university, said: "[Chimpanzees] have the same social problems that we do, they want to make friends and find mates and gain position within their society."

Members of the research team, who also came from Kyoto University in Japan and the University of Arizona, US, gave questionnaires to around 230 people who were asked to observe chimpanzees and orangutans in zoos and research centres in the US, Canada, Australia and Japan.

The survey listed about 40 to 50 personality 'items', which when grouped together make personality dimensions. The observers were instructed to rate the apes' behaviour on a one-to-seven point scale for each personality item. Previously it had been debated whether great apes truly display human-like personalities, or if these are just the anthropomorphic projections of human observers. To eliminate this possibility researchers used a statistical technique to "remove" any biases.

Adams said: "We found that controlling for these differences among observers made no difference, which suggests that the observers were not projecting their own ideas about personality onto the animals."

Weiss concluded that the research "vindicates both the view that chimpanzees have personalities and perhaps the more controversial statement that their personalities are quite similar to those of humans."

Mid-life chimps

CHIMPS experience a "mid-life crisis" and face similar social pressures and stress factors to humans, according to an international team of researchers.

Their results were published in the *Proceedings of the National Academy of Sciences* in 2012. The researchers, who included psychologists, primatologists and economists, assessed the wellbeing and happiness of a group of chimps and orangutans, and found that these were similar to the "U-shaped curve" of happiness in humans, which is high in youth, falls to a low in midlife and rises again in old age.

Talking to *BBC Nature*, Dr Alexander Weiss of the University of Edinburgh said: "What we are testing is whether the U-shaped curve can describe the association between age and wellbeing in non-human primates as it does in humans."

The study showed that humans, chimpanzees and orangutans – both male and female – have the same U-shaped curve despite differences in social roles, and the phenomenon is therefore not uniquely human.

The research subjects included 508 chimpanzees and orangutans of varying ages, from zoos, sanctuaries and research centres. They were assessed by zoo keepers, researchers, caretakers and volunteers, who had worked with the relevant ape subject for at least two years. The apes were numerically scored for wellbeing and happiness using a questionnaire based on a modified human model.

Weiss said that the similarities between humans, chimps and orangutans go beyond genetics and physiology, and that chimps face similar social pressures and stress factors to humans.

He explained: "You don't have the chimpanzee hitting mid-life and suddenly they want a bright red sports car. But there may be other things that they want like mating with more females or gaining access to more resources."

Co-author Andrew Oswald, professor of economics at the University of Warwick, has researched human happiness for more than 20 years.

He said: "One of the reasons we decided to look at ape data was that when you study humans, that U-shape is exactly the same when you adjust statistically for things like education, income and marriage." He added that it was "quite mind-blowing... to find it in apes", and concluded that "the mid-life crisis is real and it exists in... our closest biological relatives, suggesting that it is probably explained by biology and physiology."

Weiss said that mid-life crisis had previously been considered something specific to humans: "We have to look deeper into our evolutionary past and that of the common ancestors that we share with chimpanzees, orangutans and other apes."

Role-playing chimps

YOUNG female chimps use sticks as simple 'dolls' and care for them like babies, after observing mothers in their family groups, It was reported in 2010.

This behaviour was witnessed more than 100 times over 14 years of research in Kibale National Park, Uganda, and was rarely observed in males. Anthropologists believe that this behaviour evolved to make the chimps better mothers.

Study leader Richard Wrangham, a biological anthropologist at Harvard University, said: "The stick serves no immediate function. They just carry it – sometimes for a few minutes, other times for hours."

Carried sticks were shaped differently from those used as weapons or probes, and "unlike other types of stick use, carried sticks were regularly taken into day nests... where individuals rested and were sometimes seen to play casually with the stick in a manner that evoked maternal play," wrote the researchers.

This behaviour was most frequent in juveniles; once the chimps became parents stick carrying ceased.

Wrangham said that the research represented the first time wild animals of different sexes have been observed playing differently with objects.

He suggested that this supported at least some biological origin for different play between the sexes in humans.

Measuring chimps

CHIMPS can measure the volume of liquid as it is poured, and are able to gauge the difference between continuous quantities such as a pint or half pint, according to a study in 2010 at Georgia State University and published in the journal *Animal Cognition*.

Previously apes were known to differentiate only discrete (individually distinct) quantities, such as eight sweets over five, but this study, using fruit juice, showed chimps demonstrating an ability to gauge the difference between continuous quantities.

Comparative psychologist Dr Michael Beran researched the differing mental abilities of monkeys, apes and humans.

He had already shown that primates are able to keep track of how many sweets are in a container; by performing simple addition and subtraction calculations they can work out how many are added or taken away.

But liquids posed a different challenge: because liquid flows, it forms one continuous quantity which becomes larger as more liquid is added.

Beran said: "I wanted to know whether they would perform as well when they had to judge two poured amounts of juice."

He tested three chimps: two females, aged 21 and 37, and a male aged 34. In the first experiment, Beran poured different quantities of juice from a syringe into both a clear cup and opaque cup. The chimps watched as he did this, and then chose the cup with the larger quantity to drink.

Beran poured quantities measuring 100ml, 200ml, 300ml and up to 600ml into either cup, and the chimps selected the larger volume more than threequarters of the time.

When the liquid was poured into opaque containers, the chimps could see only how much was being poured, not how much had accumulated in the cup. Beran said that once the liquid was in the containers, it was out of sight. So the chimps had to remember how much juice was there, just from seeing it fall.

Then the chimps had to choose between a clear cup already containing a certain volume of juice, and another they couldn't see, but into which was poured some juice.

That meant the chimps could not take the relatively easy option of timing the pouring events, and choose whichever cup had liquid poured into it for longer. Beran explained that the chimps successfully compared the poured amount to the visible amount, and estimated which was the larger.

Then Beran varied the height from which the liquids were poured, creating a perceptual illusion that might have confused the chimps.

"I wanted to see whether the chimps overestimated the amount of juice if it was poured from higher up," he said. "This is an old favourite of the experienced bartenders of the world, where the patron gets the impression of getting more alcohol than is really true because of varying the height of the pouring."

All three chimps picked the largest amount more than 80 percent of the time, with the 21-year-old scoring a high of 86 percent.

Beran concluded: "The results support the position that chimpanzees are good mental accountants."

Culinary chimps

IN 2009 chimpanzees were seen for the first time using tools to chop up and reduce food to smaller bite-sized portions.

The journal *Primates* reported that in the Nimba Mountains of Guinea, Africa, chimps were observed using both stone and wooden cleavers together with stone anvils made from immovable rocky outcrops to process the fruit of the treculia tree, or African breadfruit. The fruits are large, tough and fibrous, weighing up to 8.5kg. They don't have a hard outer shell, but they are too big for chimps to get their jaws around and bite into.

Researchers pointed out that the chimps were not simply cracking into the fruit to get to otherwise unobtainable food, they were actively chopping up the food into more manageable portions. It was the first time wild chimpanzees had been seen using two distinct types of tool to achieve the same result.

The study was carried out by primatologist Kathelijne Koops and Professor William McGrew of the Leverhulme Centre for Human Evolutionary Studies at Cambridge University.

Koops told the BBC: "Chimpanzees across Africa vary greatly in the types of tools they use to obtain food. Some groups use stones as hammers and anvils to crack open nuts, whereas others use twigs to fish for termites. For example, nut-cracking in the Bossou chimpanzee community in Guinea involves the use of a movable hammer and anvil, and sometimes the additional use of stabilising wedges to make the anvil more level and so more efficient.

"Termite fishing in some chimpanzee communities in the Republic of Congo involves the use of a tool set, i.e. different tool components used sequentially to achieve the same goal. These chimpanzees were found to deliberately modify termite fishing probes by creating a brush-end, before using them to fish for termites."

Koops added that surprisingly, neighbouring chimps living in the nearby region of Seringbara did not process their food in this way, reinforcing the belief that tool use among apes is culturally learnt.

Musical chimps

CHIMPS are biologically programmed to appreciate pleasant music, something previously thought to be a universal human trait.

In 2009 the journal *Primates* reported on an experiment involving an infant chimpanzee who chose to listen to harmonious rather than dissonant music. This suggested to researchers that chimps are born with an innate appreciation of pleasant sounds, and that this trait evolved in the ancestors of both humans and modern apes.

Japanese researchers Tasuku Sugimoto and Kazuhide Hashiya and their colleagues at Kyushu University in Hakozaki, tested how a young captive chimp named Sakura responded to music when she was between 17 and 23 weeks old.

Sakura, abandoned by her mother, was reared by members of staff at Itozu-no-mori Park in Fukuoka. She had never been exposed to any form of music before. During the experiments the chimp, laying on a bed, had a woollen string attached to her right hand, allowing her to pull on the cord at will.

A music player and speakers were set up around her, playing melodies lasting between 38 and 63 seconds. Every time Sakura pulled on the cord, the music would be repeated.

There were six trials every week for six weeks, when the researchers played Sakura a range of tunes lasting around 20 minutes. In three of the trials, the researchers first played Sakura the more pleasant consonant music, and in the others they started with the less pleasant sounding music.

In all the sessions, Sakura pulled on the cord significantly more often to listen to the pleasurable music than to the dissonant.

Hashiya said they were surprised at how consistent the results were: "She rapidly learnt the rule of the set-up and consistently produced consonant music over dissonant music for longer duration."

The researchers believed that the discovery that an infant chimp, with no prior exposure to music, innately preferred to listen to consonant melodies could have important implications for how humans' appreciation for music evolved. Hashiya said that this is a universal attribute like language, but it was always thought to be a uniquely human trait, present even in babies just a few days old.

The researchers speculated that the chimps' preference for pleasurable melodies may serve some biological function in the wild, perhaps helping them detect other chimps' voices above other sounds.

Number crunching chimps

CHIMPS have a photographic memory far superior to ours, according to research published in *Current Biology* in 2007.

Young chimps outperformed humans in memory tests devised by Japanese scientists. The tasks involved remembering the location of numbers on a screen, and correctly recalling the sequence. Dr Tetsuro Matsuzawa of Kyoto University told the BBC: "We are still underestimating the intellectual capability of chimpanzees." He said it was hard to believe that five-year-old chimps could perform better in a memory task than adult humans.

Matsuzawa said: "Here we show for the first time that young chimpanzees have an extraordinary working memory capability for numerical recollection – better than that of human adults tested in the same apparatus, following the same procedure."

Matsuzawa and colleagues tested three pairs of mother and baby chimps against university students in a memory task involving numbers. The mothers and their five-year-old offspring had already been taught to "count" from one to nine.

During the experiment, each subject was presented with various numerals from one to nine on a touch screen monitor.

The numbers were then replaced with blank squares and the test subject had to remember which number had appeared in which location, then touch the appropriate square. In general, the young chimps performed better than their mothers and the adult humans.

The researchers then varied the amount of time that the numbers appeared on screen to compare the working memory of humans and chimps. The chimps outperformed the students in speed and accuracy when the numbers appeared only briefly on screen.

The shortest duration, 210 milliseconds, did not leave enough time for the subjects to explore the screen by eye movement which humans do when reading.

The researchers concluded that this is evidence that young chimps have a photographic memory which allows them to memorise a complex scene or pattern at a glance. This is sometimes present in human children but declines with age.

Some anthropologists believe this ability evolved because of chimps' need to memorise where different fruit, ripening at different times, can be found within their territory.

Stone throwing chimp

SANTINO, a male chimp at Furuvik Zoo near Stockholm, Sweden, had a habit of throwing stones at visitors, demonstrating that chimps can plan for future events.

According to a report in the journal *Current Biology* in 2009, Santino apparently had planned hundreds of stone-throwing attacks on zoo visitors. Keepers noticed that the chimp collected and stored stones that he would later use as missiles. The chimp also learned to recognise how and when parts of his concrete enclosure could be pulled apart to make further projectiles.

Santino collected the stones while he was in a calm state, before the zoo opened in the morning, but it wasn't until much later that he threw the stones at visitors while he was in an agitated state during dominance displays.

This suggested that Santino was planning in advance and anticipating how he would feel later – an ability that had been difficult to prove in animals, according to the author of the research, Mathias Osvath, a cognitive scientist from Lund University in Sweden.

Zoo staff had discovered caches of stones in the section of the enclosure facing the public viewing area and had removed hundreds of them, guessing they were to be aimed at visitors. Out of the tourist season, Santino neither hoarded nor hurled the projectiles.

Santino had also apparently learned how to spot weak parts of the concrete 'boulders' in the centre of the enclosure. When water seeped into cracks in the concrete and froze, portions became detached and made a hollow sound when tapped.

Santino was observed gently knocking on the 'boulders', hitting harder to detach bits that were loosened and adding those to his stashes of ammunition.

Film director chimps

IN 2010 the BBC aired a film made entirely by chimps. The idea was conceived by primatologist Betsy Herrelko, as part of her research into how chimpanzees perceive the world and one another.

Herrelko introduced 11 chimps at Edinburgh Zoo to video technology over an 18 month period, then set the chimps two challenges. The first was to learn how to use a touchscreen to select different videos so she could find out which types of images the chimps preferred to watch. The second challenge was to use a 'chimpcam', a recording camera housed in a chimp-proof box.

The chimps' enclosure was one of the largest of its kind in the world, containing three interlinked outdoor arenas plus a series of smaller rooms in which the apes could be studied by the researchers.

After a couple of setbacks caused by two males vying for dominance, the chimps eventually learned how to operate the touchscreen and were able to choose which videos they liked best: ones showing their outside enclosure or the food preparation room.

After this was mastered, the chimps were given the chimpcam. They played with it and carried it around the enclosure, then soon became interested in the camera view screen on the chimpcam box, watching what happened as they moved the box around, filming new images. Researchers noticed that they were usually more interested in the chimpcam viewfinder than they were in the touchscreen in the research room.

The resulting film *Chimpcam* was screened as part of a *Natural World* programme shown on BBC2 in January 2010.

Gesturing chimps

ONLY humans and chimps have a system of communication where individuals deliberately send a message to another, according to Dr Catherine Hobaiter from the University of St Andrews.

She said that the wild chimps she studied communicated 19 specific messages to one another with a "lexicon" of 66 gestures.

Hobaiter and other scientists followed and filmed communities of chimps in Uganda, and examined more than 5,000 incidents of these meaningful exchanges. Hobaiter said that this was the only form of intentional communication to be recorded in the animal kingdom.

"That's what's so amazing about chimp gestures," she said.

Chimps will check to see if they have the attention of the animal with which they wish to communicate. Although many gestures are very subtle, some of the footage captured by the researchers shows very clearly what the chimps mean to convey.

In one clip, a mother presents her foot to her whimpering offspring, signalling: "Climb on me". The young chimp immediately jumps on to its mother's back and they travel off together.

There is a crucial difference between calls and gestures, Hobaiter added. "It's a bit like if you pick up a hot cup of coffee and you scream and blow on your fingers. I can understand from that that the coffee was hot, but you didn't necessarily intend to communicate that to me."

It appears that some of the chimps' gestures are unambiguous, always used to convey one particular meaning. An example is leaf clipping, where a chimp takes small bites from leaves to encourage sexual attention. But many other gestures appear to be ambiguous. For instance a grab can mean "Stop that," "Climb on me," or "Move away".

Hobaiter said: "The big message is that there is another species out there that is meaningful in its communication, so that's not unique to humans. I don't think we're quite as set apart as we would perhaps like to think we are."

Although previous research has revealed that apes and monkeys can understand complex information from another animal's call, the animals do not appear to use their voices intentionally to communicate messages.

The research was published in *Current Biology* in 2014.

Head-shaking chimps

BONOBOS (pygmy chimps) have been observed appearing to say 'no' by shaking their heads, and a mother was seen doing this to stop her infant playing with its food.

According to a report in the journal *Primates* in 2010 several instances of this type of head shaking were observed at six European zoos by researcher Christel Schneider and her colleagues from the Max Planck Institute for Evolutionary Anthropology in Leipzig, Germany.

On a number of occasions, bonobos were filmed using side-to-side head movements to prevent others from doing something they did not want them to do.

During the study, researchers witnessed four individual bonobos shaking their heads in this way on 13 different occasions. It is thought this may reflect an early precursor to head-shaking behaviour amongst humans.

Previously bonobos and chimpanzees had been observed using

head gestures such as nodding, bowing and shaking to communicate with other group members, and bonobos had been seen using head-shaking to initiate interactions with other members of the group, such as playing, but this was the first study to film and observe an ape shaking its head in a negative context to stop or prevent behaviour in another individual.

Researchers said that more detailed research was needed to fully establish the functional role of all forms of head gestures across ape species.

"There is no other creature that so charms and fascinates the beholder as do these little effigies of the human race."

R L Garner (1896)

Natural chimps

BETWEEN six and eight million years ago an ape ancestor split into two groups, one the forerunner of humans, the other of chimpanzees. Over the subsequent millennia the two groups split many more times, diverging and evolving further into many different species, most now extinct.

Remaining species today include humans (homo sapiens) now numbering around seven billion, and chimpanzees (pan troglodytes), approximately 150,000 living naturally in the wild at time of writing, and diminishing fast.

The other two surviving great apes, gorillas (two species: gorilla gorilla and gorilla beringei) and orangutans (pongo), travelled a separate evolutionary path, still retaining many similarities to humans. (Some anthropologists suggest there are four remaining great apes, including humans.) But it's the chimpanzee who resembles man most closely, both physically and culturally, sharing nearly 99 percent of our DNA.

Chimpanzees belong to a single species which is sometimes subdivided into four races: bonobos (formerly called pygmy chimpanzees) and three groups of common chimpanzees, though some primatologists regard all common chimps as one race. They live in restricted areas of Africa and extend east as far as Tanzania.

The three common groups are separated by habitat, consisting of secondary dry woodland savannah, grassland and tropical rain forest. (Even though chimps' habitat is often near water, they cannot swim, due to the structure and density of their bodies.) But these areas have been severely depleted.

Neither ape nor human

A STUDY in 2013 challenged the perception that the last common ancestor of man and apes resembled today's chimpanzee. Research published in the journal *Nature Communications* concluded that this ancestor was in fact an ape unlike any that exists today.

From this ancestor, said the study, humans and modern day apes evolved in two completely different directions. Anatomical scientist Wergio Almecija of the Stony Brook University Medical Center in New York, said: "The majority of palaeoanthropologists tend to assume that the last common ancestor of chimps and humans looked like a chimp. However, there is growing evidence suggesting that the ... great apes are not 'living time machines' reflecting our past, but that they have also evolved since their lineage split from that of humans millions of years ago."

Almecija and his team based their conclusions on the study of a femur from "Millennium Man" (scientific name Orrorin Tugenensis), an ape which lived in Kenya six million years ago. This was the first study to compare Millennium Man's physiology not only with humans and living apes, but with fossil apes from the Miocine period 23 to 5.3 million years ago.

Millennium Man climbed trees and walked upright, and the scientists placed him in an evolutionary bracket between the unidentified common human-ape ancestor and the line that led to modern homo sapiens.

They believe that the common ancestor was similar to Orrorin but different to modern chimps, which diverged with humans about 6-8 million years ago.

It is estimated that 50 years ago there were a million chimps living in Africa. They used to inhabit 25 countries throughout tropical Africa but chimps are now extinct in five of those countries and endangered in five others.

However, in February 2014 anthropologists discovered a previously undetected group of chimps – thought to number tens of thousands – in remote forests in the north of the Democratic Republic of the Congo and on the border of the central African Republic. The chimps are larger than average and, unusually, build nests on the ground, not in the tree tops.

Locomotion

Chimps can travel equally well along the ground or through the trees. They run on all fours with their weight carried on their feet and on the backs of their knuckles. Their arms are longer than their legs and they scale trees by holding the trunk with their arms and pushing with their feet. They use both hands and feet to cling to branches,

Chimpanzees mainly walk with their weight carried on their feet and on the backs of their knuckles.

and sometimes move short distances through the trees by swinging from branch to branch with their arms.

However, one group is known to behave differently. The habitat of the chimps of Fongoli in Senegal is largely grasslands and to adapt to these conditions they have become more bipedal (walking upright). Primatologist Jill Pruetz believes the way these chimps have evolved possibly shows how the ancestors of humans changed as they left the forests and stepped out onto the savannah grasslands.

Tool use

Chimps are the most proficient tool-makers after man, and use sticks and stones as weapons and probe ant nests with sticks, sometimes after having broken and filed them to size. Chimps from different parts of Africa have different cultural traditions and will learn different skills to those in other areas, e.g. 'fishing' for termites or using a rock as a hammer on a rock anvil (see 'Culinary chimps' on page 83).

Primatologist Jane Goodall noted that a probe may also be used to investigate something worrying like a dead python. And she saw chimps use leaves as toilet paper, to wipe wounds or remove mud from food. They also used stout sticks as levers, to enlarge the opening of an underground bees' nest. One chimp even used a twig as a toothpick.

Chimps' predominant diet is fruit, plus some vegetables, and because different trees produce fruit at different times, and areas of plentiful availability may be widely spaced it is thought this predisposes them to have good memories (see 'Number crunching chimps' on page 86). In the rain forests they climb trees to pick ripe fruits in season, or leaves when fruit is in short supply. They have also been known to use plants with medicinal value to self-medicate. When vegetation is scarce they eat termites and kill and eat other animals, sometimes even monkeys. Chimps drink by dipping a hand into water and licking it or using a leaf as a 'sponge' to soak up water.

Group politics

Chimps have the most complex social system of any ape other than humans. They communicate with one another through a complex, subtle system of vocalisations, facial expressions, body postures and gestures (see 'Gesturing chimps' on page 89).

They live in large groups of 15 to 120 individuals in a highly organised community with a home range varying in area from about eight square miles, if food is abundant, up to 30 square miles in savanna woodlands. Sometimes the group will split into smaller sub-groups.

Each group is headed by an alpha male and he often relies on a second-in-command to keep control, and each chimp within the group has a particular social status. A core group of related males regularly patrols the boundaries of the community's territory.

The males establish their rank by displays of dominance; with hair erect, they sway rhythmically backwards and forwards, hooting loudly. They rush about, waving branches, uprooting plants or throwing rocks. Lower ranking chimps crouch or bob in front of the dominant male, or make way when they meet.

When excited, as when food is found, adult males drum on the buttress roots of trees or on the ground, and other chimps join in with a loud hooting chorus. This drumming has also been observed during thunderstorms.

Females also have a hierarchy with an alpha female at the top. When a low ranking female becomes a mother she is often given more respect and thus rises up the social scale.

Childcare

Pregnancy lasts 230-260 days, similar to that of humans. At birth, a chimp weighs about four pounds and has a white tuft of fur on his or her rump (this is thought to be a signal to older chimps to treat them with care). Chimps generally give birth to a single infant each pregnancy and mothers and their young tend to remain together at the heart of each community; where groups overlap aggression between males can occur. Baby chimps cling to their mothers' backs while travelling and are weaned at approximately four years, but generally

Babies cling on to their mothers' backs while travelling.

Females tend to retain a strong association with their mothers and will 'help' with younger siblings.

stay with their mothers until they are about six to eight years old. They still remain close until, usually about 10 years old, youngsters leave their mothers for progressively longer periods. Jane Goodall lists the following milestones in her book *In The Shadow of Man*:

"Sucks thumb at two months; first piece of solid food at four months; starts to ride on mother's back at five months; starts to use tools at three years; loses milk teeth at six; first infant born [when mother is] about 11 or 12 years. Males becomes fully socially mature about 15 years."

Young males soon join other adults, but females tend to retain a stronger association with their mothers. They will often 'help' with younger siblings, sometimes carrying the baby on their backs like their mother. (See 'Role playing chimps' on page 80.)

Goodall continues: "Chimps make their beds from a 'nest' of interwoven or layered leafy branches, which form a platform for the night. Every evening at dusk the chimps build fresh nests, up to 100ft above the ground, and they often sleep for up to 12 hours. Young chimps watch their mothers carefully and learn to do the same." Mothers may enjoy life-long bonds with their adult sons and daughters.

Standing upright on two legs, an adult chimp may reach over four feet in height and weigh as much as 150 lbs.

Friendship

Like humans, chimps are extremely sociable. When they greet each other they will hold out a hand (they also seem to favour the right) to show they are a friend, and they cement friendships by grooming each other. (Some anthropologists believe we demonstrate a long ago link with this kind of behaviour in our fondness for hair and beauty parlours.) Close social relationships are common throughout life between members of the same family, but near relatives rarely mate.

In 2013 Jorg Massen, a researcher at Vienna University confirmed that chimps have the same instinct as humans to form enduring relationships with "best friends". Like humans, chimps develop lasting same-sex friendships based largely on personality similarities. Some chimps are far better at making friends than others and these individuals seem to be more likely to survive and thrive.

Chimps have the same instinct as humans to form enduring relationships with "best friends".

Vocalising and communication

Chimps are the noisiest of the great apes and have a wide variety of calls and gestures. They demonstrate their friendships by gentle grunting or panting, mutual grooming, hand-holding or embracing. A low hoot is a warning to others and a loud bark is an indication of threat. Quarrels may be accompanied by screams of rage or fear. Chimps also have a range of facial expressions by which they communicate.

Human-like traits

- Chimps use facial expressions to convey emotions.

- Chimps have emotions similar to those we call joy, anger, grief, sorrow, pleasure, boredom, and depression. They also comfort and reassure one another by kissing and embracing.

- Chimps have 32 teeth, the same as humans.

- Chimps' body temperature is the same as humans, at 98.6 degrees.

- The senses of sight, taste, and hearing are similar to those of humans.

- Chimps have opposable thumbs, like humans, as well as opposable big toes, so they can use both their hands and feet to climb and grab objects.

- While humans have blood types A, B, O and AB, chimps have only A or O.

- Many older chimps suffer from cardiac disease and, in captivity, are given the same medications that humans take for heart conditions.

(Information courtesy of Save The Chimps.)

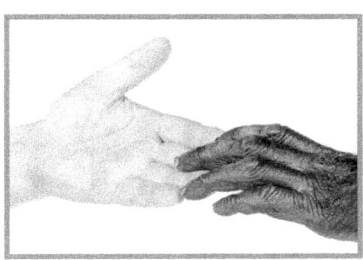

Postscript

SOME time ago I was channel hopping and by chance came upon a TV programme highlighting the lives of rescued apes and monkeys at a sanctuary.

My attention was taken by the chimps in particular; it was the first time I had seen them close up, behaving naturally in social groups, and was struck by the similarity to humans in their behaviour; at the same time I was amused by their antics.

Then the commentary alerted me to the fact that most of these chimps had originally been abused and frightened individuals who had been transformed into well-adjusted and happy members of their adopted families, thanks to the patience and dedication of the sanctuary staff.

One scene featured three baby chimps, just a few months old, who had lost their mothers. They were too frightened to leave the safety of the inside living area and had been left behind by their older companions who were running and playing outside. One baby was hugging her bedding straw like a human child's comfort blanket, pushing a bundle of it before her as she cautiously moved about. She was evidently more courageous than the other two and she took the lead, with another baby holding on behind with arms round the first's waist, and the third doing the same, creating a shuffling threesome locked together behind the reassuring straw.

A couple of years later I visited the same sanctuary and, looking through the window of an enclosure, saw two chimps sitting on a radiator with their backs to the visitors, looking out of the window at the cold November day. A third chimp approached and the seated

... how anyone could doubt that the chimpanzee species demonstrate empathy and social awareness...

two shuffled up to make room, one holding out an arm to welcome the newcomer and gather him or her closer. I wondered if these were the same babies, now two years older, more confident and assimilated into their social group. And I questioned how anyone could doubt that the chimpanzee species demonstrate empathy and social awareness and that a life spent isolated away from their own kind would be devastating and cruel.

It was these two observations in particular which set me on the path to find out more about our closest living relative and ultimately resulted in the publication of this book.

Julie Norton

Other books by Julie Norton:

Nice Nipper

Where mother and daughter find themselves travelling back in time together to Marylebone, London in the 1920s... an unusual take on the effects of Alzheimer's disease.

by the late Mira Harmer
and her daughter Julie Norton

A cup of tea that is forever England

Lighthearted tales of working class family life in 1960s London originally published in the Morning Star newspaper.

by Mira Harmer
Edited by Julie Norton

Available from Amazon Books
Produced by www.branchwoodpublishing.co.uk